Centerlined

henry j. sienkiewicz

All of the best,
Henry Sienkiewicz

© 2006 Henry J. Sienkiewicz
All Rights Reserved.

No part of this publication may be reproduced, stored in a retrieval system, or transmitted, in any form or by any means, electronic, mechanical, photocopying, recording, or otherwise, without the written permission of the author.

First published by Dog Ear Publishing
4010 W. 86th Street, Ste H
Indianapolis, IN 46268
www.dogearpublishing.net

dog ear
PUBLISHING

ISBN: 1-59858-186-4

This book is printed on acid-free paper.

Printed in the United States of America

Table of Contents

Chapter 1:	Seeing Your Centerline	1
Chapter 2:	Understanding Your Centerline	5
Chapter 3:	It Is Your Own Centerline	8
Chapter 4:	Framing	12
Chapter 5:	The Impact of the Frame	14
Chapter 6:	Framing Our Centerline	16
Chapter 7:	Breaking Our Frames	19
Chapter 8:	Within Our Own Centerline	21
Chapter 9:	Our Points Within	23
Chapter 10:	Recognizing Our Own Centerline	28
Chapter 11:	An Integrated Journey	30
Chapter 12:	Seeing Other Centerlines	32
Chapter 13:	Commonality	34
Chapter 14:	Searching For Commonality	37
Chapter 15:	Finding Commonality	39
Chapter 16:	Common Places	40
Chapter 17:	Challenges to Commonality	42
Chapter 18:	Reflection, Not Obsession	44
Chapter 19:	Activity vs. Action	46
Chapter 20:	Risk	48
Chapter 21:	Fear	49
Chapter 22:	Translucence	51
Chapter 23:	Grounding Our Centerline	54
Chapter 24:	Continual Revelations	57
Chapter 25:	False Surety	59
Chapter 26:	Centerlining Love	60
Chapter 27:	Centerlined Rules?	64
Chapter 28:	Self Centerlines	66
Chapter 29:	Organizational Centerlines	74
Chapter 30:	Communicating Our Centerlines	82
Chapter 31:	The Centerline Paradox	85
Chapter 32:	Centerlined Leadership: No Heroes, Friars, or Lords	87
Chapter 33:	Approaches to Living a Centerline	93
Chapter 34:	Drawing Your Centerline	101
Works Consulted		103
Discussion Group Questions		113

Chapter 1

Seeing Your Centerline

"All children are artists. The problem is how to remain an artist once he grows up."
- Pablo Picasso

The flash of understanding came as I sat babysitting two of my nieces. Crayons in hand, they were intent on putting their vision onto the paper in front of them. Peacefully drawing away, every few minutes they had a new work of art for my refrigerator. I could not help comparing their focus and execution to the endless series of strategy meetings that I had participated in during the previous two weeks.

I marveled at how easily my nieces were able to put their vision down on a blank piece of paper. In contrast, I routinely see how difficult it is for the rest of us to understand our own perspectives and do the same. I struggled to understand why this was the case.

I had just returned to my job after a year-long military reserve mobilization. It's not often we get the opportunity to step outside of our normal roles, and I had taken advantage of such an opportunity. Because initially I had not been in a direct leadership role, I was finally able to have the time to think. I had taken that year to reflect.

The mobilization itself was unplanned, and not particularly wanted. During the previous two years, I had already performed a great deal of reserve duty. In the aftermath of September 11th, my team and I had spent many long months doing classified analysis work. I was enjoying my position at an information technology company. Opening the mobilization letter that November morning really spoiled my breakfast.

Fortunately, the tour went well. I was never in harm's way. I remembered the reasons that I enjoyed being a military officer—the ethos of duty and the sense of comradeship. I remembered the reasons why I preferred being a citizen soldier—my preference for established roots within a community.

In a departure from my normal focus on managing technology, my military duties concentrated on manpower management, organizational structures, outsourcing, and detainee abuse investigations. This duty focus, though, nicely complemented those things I wanted to concentrate on. I was able to give a great deal of thought to how we develop our own perspectives and how we can find a cohesive way to look at the world. I sought to understand our connections with each other and structure ways in which we can better relate to each other. I gained a much greater appreciation of all of the efforts that human resources professionals routinely go through.

While watching my nieces draw, I noticed something interesting. The younger one knew what she wanted to draw. She had an inclusive, holistic perspective about her art and had the ability to express it. She knew what the focus and theme of her picture should be and she could link those together in a meaningful fashion.

Intuitively, she understood that to communicate her vision she had to put herself—her ideas and her perspectives—into that drawing. She had an approach to managing the tension between the existing state found on that blank piece of paper and the evolving state found within her mind.

I observed how she took things that were concrete only to her and placed them outside herself. She gave them structure and put them into a greater context. Her approach of simultaneously centering herself within and outside her picture was the key to what I was struggling with. Through her drawings, she gave her ideas a cohesive form. Her form worked not only for herself but for others.

Most of us have lost this ability. We sit in meetings, scratching out logos and halfway listening to slogans *ad nauseam*. We hear the droning of goal setting and vision creation. We engage in team-building exercises that serve only to highlight our differences. We doodle, but we don't draw.

We feel the emptiness of these activities; we feel alienation in not understanding what our role is; we feel anxiety about the future. When we look below the surface, we find that these feelings come from something very profound but routinely unrecognized. We only see doodles and not drawings.

We suffer from a basic confusion and inability to recognize and integrate our principles and actions; we can't seem to recognize and integrate other viewpoints. We end up struggling, not only with the "who" or "what" we are, but "how" we live and relate to others.

Why is it that we can't seem to have a holistic, inclusive perspective about our daily life? How can we unify thought and action in our daily activities? Why can't we have conversations that cut through the veils surrounding each of us? How do we center ourselves both within and outside ourselves, draw our own pictures and connect with others?

I don't think that these expectations are unrealistic. As I thought these topics through, I realized that one answer involves the process of Centerlining. *Centerlining* is a method of reflecting and acting on your core values. Your Centerline is the expression of your values. You reflectively and actively link them all together into a coherent framework. You start to draw.

We all recognize that our lives are a journey, a continual process of achieving some semblance of order for both ourselves and our community from a backdrop of noise and nonsense. A realized Centerline gives us a way to balance our life. It allows us to create and conserve simultaneously. When we are Centerlining, we model a holistic perspective on life. We recognize our complexities and priorities. We understand our fundamental similarities with others. We embrace a continual revelation. We center ourselves in love.

Centerlining is pragmatic, with some specific approaches that we can take. But Centerlining is also idealistic. We continue to dream as we look to universal ideals and put them within our daily reality.

Our Centerline journey involves understanding ourselves, recognizing why we hold particular views, candidly reassessing our beliefs, integrating our values, establishing common ground with others, and finding ways to live an actively Centerlined life.

The key points of this Centerlined approach to life are:

- Explicitly balancing complex, competing interests
- Integrating and communicating *our* values
- Finding our sense of community, our "*we*"
- Linking ourselves together with commonality and mutual respect
- Grounding our communities in love
- Finding meaningful ways to act

We are fortunate to live in a time of almost infinite possibilities. Centerlining helps us identify and act on those things that matter. It is a relatively straightforward concept for what can be the difficult matter of thinking about, finding, and expressing our own perspective on life. It is neither a short nor easy process. We cannot expect instant changes and immediate results. Centerlining calls us to step back, reflect, and act.

By Centerlining, we can figure out and communicate about what makes us tick, and provide a means to bring this about in daily life. To borrow a phrase from John Dewey, Centerlining is a "philosophy of practical activity." It is an approach that creates commonality, requires candor, embraces curiosity, and fosters consistency.

Centerlining is a model for our search for perspective, our search for that unification of the transcendental and the concrete. The process forward gives a way to think through our values, to balance competing interests explicitly, to link them together, to communicate them, and to live them. My niece's art is almost always beautiful, for her drawings are a spontaneous expression of this unity.

Chapter 2

Understanding Your Centerline

"We don't see things as they are; we see them as we are."
- Anaïs Nin

Every second of our lives, a multitude of things happen to us. Some of them are major, some minor, some tangible, and some intangible. Some of these things have meaning for us, but many are relatively unimportant. In experiencing these things, we continually, unconsciously, separate the wheat from the chaff.

This white noise contains the notes for our music of creation. We all cull meaning from background noise. In so doing, we try to identify our own critical issues. We search for those things that highlight our values and our sense of self, those things on which we will not compromise. Centerlining is a way to identify, link together, and communicate those things that we value most.

Centerlining originated as a conceptual technique to communicate crucial tasks within organizations. In these traditional hierarchical environments, leaders have their particular series of goals, targets, and objectives. Further, they have multiple competing interests and priorities. These interests, values, and goals are frequently scattered about with no unifying rhyme or reason.

FIGURE 1: Scattered Multiple Competing Interests and Priorities

If they succeeded in linking these things in some meaningful order, then they established a Centerline. Their Centerline provided a powerful framework that joined together the things that would have to happen for them to be considered successful. Their vision provided a vivid drawing of their ideas and ideals. Success here could be as simple as an increase in share prices or successful delivery of a particular product, or as complex as the discovery of innovative ways to solve a crisis.

FIGURE 2: Linking Priorities and Interests

Sadly, most visions and perspectives are merely buzzword-compliant doodles. They employ current catchphrases and turns of the tongue that may make you pause but don't make you think and act. They are not balanced nor do they embody real values.

I constantly see "inspirational" posters that have less depth than the average fortune cookie, or mission statements that are so vapid that they could have come off the back of a box of cereal. I've listened to roomfuls of very highly paid executives ponder the meaning of a single word within a vision statement for hours, while their team members spend years without ever getting any meaningful feedback. Their buzzword-induced haze clouds the organization's thoughts and actions. These "accomplishments" merely deal with the trivial.

Sometimes, though, their message works. It's concise, clear, inspiring, unifying, consistent, and balanced. You see the things that really matter. You understand how and why they complement each other. You know how one action impacts others. You embrace messages that are clearly formulated and readily understood, and which give rise to meaningful action. The message is Centerlined.

In communicating an organizational Centerline, I prefer to use only a few words that capture our vision and direction, and our place in it as organizations and as individuals. I like simple phrases that resonate with life and meaning to describe my own Centerline. An expressed Centerline may be a few "bullets" on a PowerPoint presentation or a simple drawing like my nieces routinely give me.

Our own journey is an attempt to find a similar coherent perspective—our own Centerline. Our perspective has to be not only clear and concise, but also truly Centerlined. As we develop our understanding, most of us seek reasons for our beliefs. We routinely try to find the palettes and canvas that help us make sense of our lives and relate ourselves with others.

I would challenge you to take a few minutes and jot down four components of your life. These should be aspects that cross the various elements of your life—your family, your career, your religion, your health—that you believe are truly important. Think about why they are important to you and how you connect them together.

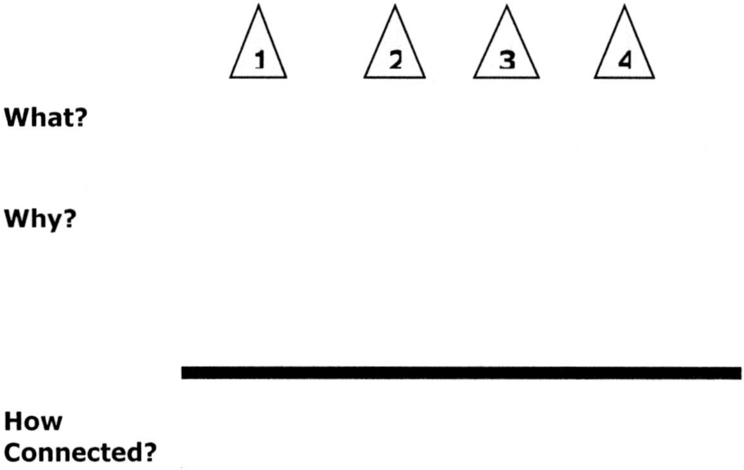

△1 △2 △3 △4

What?

Why?

How Connected?

FIGURE 3: Identifying and Linking Components

Chapter 3

It Is Your Own Centerline

"I know who I am and who I may be, if I choose."
- *Miguel de Cervantes*

In this time of change, we are increasingly pushed to accept absolute certainty in our lives, accepting authoritarianism in religion, science, and politics. Brokers behind the political landscape force polarization. Radical fundamentalists of every creed, throughout the world, push their brand of absolutism.

Although initially comforting, this authoritarianism cannot satisfy our innate needs. We realize that these singular, simplistic beliefs do not work in a life that is full and complex, a world that is multi-polar. Our Centerline has to reflect multiple points of definition and methods of interaction rather than absolute definitions.

We can cross the chasm that separates simplistic and complex beliefs as we start to model and develop our Centerlines. We can cross from a child-like state of being defined by others to a more self-realized state. We know that we all can think independently; we don't all march to the same drummer. We have the right to question. We have the right to expect well-reasoned, logical discourse as we find our answers.

In the pragmatist school of thought, Charles Pierce's theory of inquiry stands as one attempt to show how the tensions between reflection and action—in traditional terms, *theoria* and *praxis*—can be unified in a community of inquiry. Each member of the community becomes committed to a continuous cycle of reflection and self-critical activity.

To some degree, we all already engage in this cycle. The difference here is that our Centerlines are explicit and entered into with a sense of awareness. Through self-awareness and development, everyone can understand their "frame" and create their own intentional Centerline.

Again, reflect upon those four components that you identified in Chapter 3. Think for a few more minutes about why they are particularly important. What makes them crucial to your sense of your self? Why do they matter? What influences them?

1

- **Family Influences**
- **Social Influences**
- **Religious Influences**
- **Work Influences**

2

- **Family Influences**
- **Social Influences**
- **Religious Influences**
- **Work Influences**

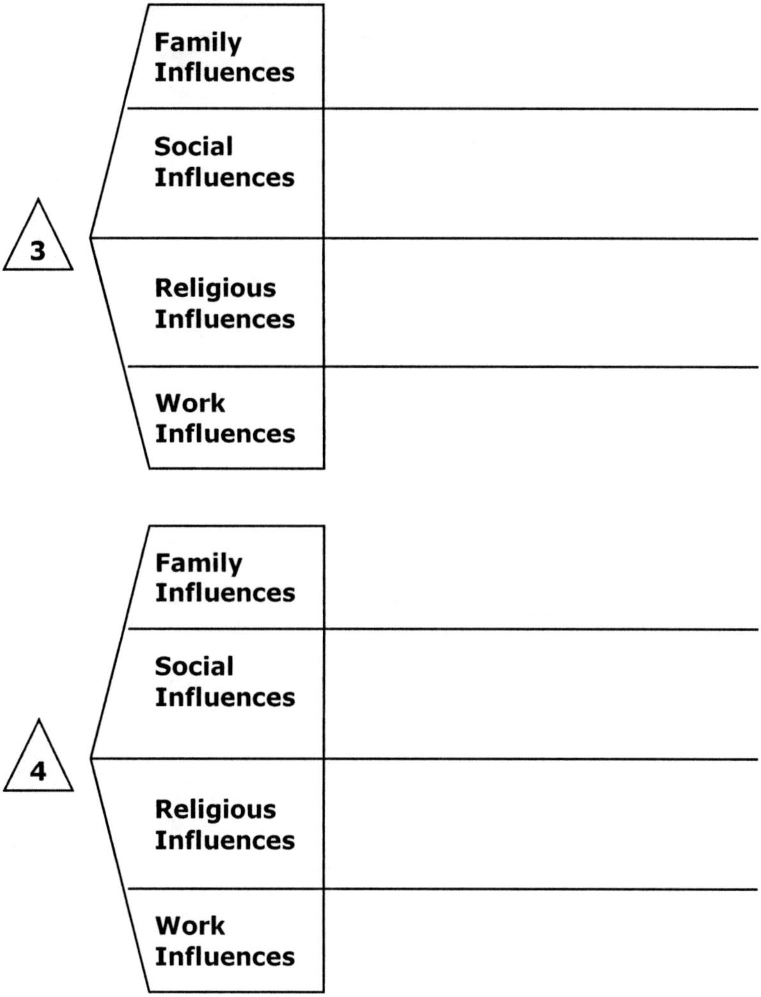

3

- **Family Influences** _____
- **Social Influences** _____
- **Religious Influences** _____
- **Work Influences** _____

4

- **Family Influences** _____
- **Social Influences** _____
- **Religious Influences** _____
- **Work Influences** _____

FIGURE 4: Identifying What Influences You and Why It Influences You

Chapter 4

Framing

> *"I asked the whole frame of the world about my God, and he answered, 'I am not He, but He made me.'"*
> - Saint Augustine

Our life is framed by our mental images, our perceptions, our beliefs, our experiences, our dreams, and a host of other features. A simple and widely accepted definition of *framing* is that it is the way something is put together or organized. As a supporting or shaping structure, a frame gives a basic arrangement to the whole and delineates borders.

One example of extreme framing is in the "happiest place on Earth"—Disney. As we enter into the Disney experience we find an all-encompassing world where every emotion is programmed, each visual impression structured, and every note part of a greater soundtrack. I have spent many days within the Disney theme parks with my nieces, family, friends, and colleagues. The experience overwhelms every sense. Disney's framing establishes boundaries that holistically unify all possible experiences onto a single stage.

The unique aspect is that Disney's framing is visible. We can examine the frames that Disney has established. We can see the structure and form and we know why a boundary is set up in a particular fashion.

Our ability to recognize and, in turn, analyze the Disney frame is a tool that can be used in our daily lives. In the same fashion that we come to understand the Disney frame, we can examine the cultural and organizational frames surrounding us.

In our daily life, we routinely establish our own boundaries and structures. We frame ourselves as we formally profess our faith or swear an oath of allegiance. Christians confess either the Apostolic or Nicene Creeds on a regular basis. These Creeds very clearly frame their religious outlooks. Service members offer an oath, which frames the conditions of their service.

With practice and encouragement, we can recognize the cultural and organizational frames that provide the structure for our macroculture. We can see how society's Centerline provides its linkages.

What we fail to realize is that everything we do is bordered by a frame. We don't stop and think about why we choose to do a particular thing or what influences us to move in a certain direction. We don't see the impact our frames have on our daily lives and we don't realize that the frames are of our own creation.

Chapter 5

The Impact of the Frame

*"You use a glass mirror to see your face;
you use works of art to see your soul."*
- George Bernard Shaw

I have never been talented enough to frame art myself. My dad was that talented; he used to stretch canvas for a sister, a commercial artist. He taught me that the frames themselves significantly impact our perception of the art.

We get caught up in the attributes of the frame. We let our existing filters dictate our perceptions. The packaging overshadows the content.

A freshly painted canvas could be of anything. Yet what we perceive greatly changes depending upon the color and shape of its frame. A canvas with a dark-green frame has a very different hue than a canvas with a bright-red frame. A simple, minimalist frame offers very different highlights than those of an art deco frame.

Works of art are affected by their physical picture frame. Frames allow for the expression of "other" meanings. A flimsy plastic frame connotes a cheap copy or something not very worthy. An elaborate frame inspires us to surround the art with security as we gently place it into a gallery; however, elaborate frames on second-rate pieces give a false sense of worth.

It is not that the frame or the medium is the message; rather, the frame is part of the message. In the words of a friend of mine, the outside framework helps us to figure out what is on the inside; it allows for insights into an art piece or a soul. A realized Centerline helps us recognize ourselves and our frames, and others and their frames.

I have a great friend who made his living moving and hanging art. Going with him to art galleries or the Arts

Club of Washington is always an adventure. His professional critiques continue to challenge and enlighten me. Routinely, he has tutored me about the artworks surrounding us. Without his mentorship I could easily walk through the exhibits, knowing that the artist was trying to communicate something but never quite grasping what he was trying to communicate.

This friend's ability to break through my preexisting frames has allowed me to see the layered influences from various movements on a particular piece, and to see how the piece's meaning changes based upon the context and time.

He has also railed at me about the placement of art within my home. Over the years, I have adjusted the pieces according to his suggestions. And, not surprisingly, it has worked. He is able to change my perceptions and allow me to see a different way to hang and, in a sense, frame my art.

This tutoring allowed me to understand why I had certain perceptions. I could apply these lessons to identifying the various layers and horizons of my understanding in all aspects of my life. I was able to see the depth, nuances, and shadows of my beliefs and the beliefs of others.

Chapter 6

Framing Our Centerline

"Principles and rules are intended to provide a thinking man with a frame of reference."
— *Karl von Clausewitz*

Society has its own frame, its own Centerline. But, as Tip O'Neill once said, "All politics is local." And the way that we live our lives is also local.

In the same way that Disney intentionally frames and builds a stage for our experience within one of their parks, we can create the frame for our own stage. Although we may have similar experiences, the space that we live in is uniquely our own. Our life is localized to ourselves.

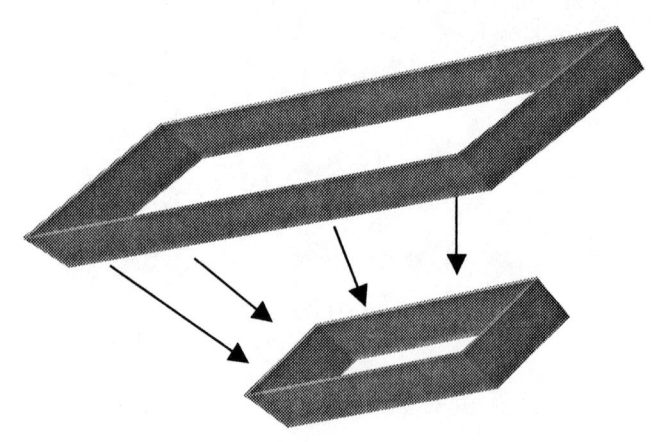

FIGURE 5: Our Part of Society's Frame

As we live in our own subset of the greater whole, we create our own microcultures. We recognize that although society has its own structure and functions, we relate and react to these things in our own fashion. We react locally as we use the macroculture's Centerlines as reference points.

For our microculture to be effectively framed and realized, our Centerlines must be well thought out. We must deliberately establish our linkages by answering the "why," "so what," "what's in it for me," and "what's in it for others." The question "How does this apply to me?" is answered. A clear, consistent vision establishes a future path with our Centerlines as guidelines.

In the world of venture capital and investor development, many businessmen and women have rehearsed an "elevator pitch." This pitch is a short description, lasting as long as an elevator ride, which summarizes a company's history, its business, its competitors, and why someone should invest in it.

Centerlining necessitates that we develop a similar elevator pitch, an elevator pitch of the self. We end up finding ways to communicate our thoughts and values actively, make them solid, and give them shape. Our Centerlining helps us to clarify our thoughts and feelings and provides us with a framework to give them shape and let us take action.

Our elevator pitch includes our sense of self, our sense of society, our sense of service, and our sense of our soul. We establish who we are, what our values are, why we hold those values, and how we give and relate to our community. What is your elevator pitch? What are your reflections on your frames?

Your Centerline can assist in your journey. You can challenge your preexisting ideas and reground them; you can surround yourself with things that inspire you; you can choose to surround yourself with people who can help you accept the risks and fears in your life.

Centerlining helps us define the frame of our microculture as we highlight where we have placed the limits to our perspectives. We look for the touch points within the macroculture and relate them to our microculture. In the creation of our self and organizational Centerlines, we use Centerlines to shape the range of discussions and the way in which we frame meaning.

However, these externalities are mere reflections. They can help you *see* what is happening. They don't actually *do* anything. In order to live fully, you have to reflect continually upon, your beliefs and your life. As you review, reflect upon and revalidate your Centerline, you may need to modify your frame.

Chapter 7

Breaking Our Frames

"We are not permitted to choose the frame of our destiny. But what we put into it is ours."
- *Dag Hammarskjöld*

Sitting in the misery that is a Washington, D.C. rush hour, I can easily rationalize altering my commute home and pass by the gym; however, when I stop regularly going to the gym, I can feel my body changing. I gain weight, get sluggish, stiffen up. This sluggishness becomes my new norm, although I know it's not beneficial to me.

Sitting in my office or at home, I can also easily rationalize accepting the immediate answers to the questions at hand. However, when I stop challenging my preconceived notions, I can perceive my thoughts becoming less rigorous, growing flabby and sluggish. As with my physical state, my mental muscles can begin to atrophy. I know that neither state is beneficial or right.

It is easy to fall into both states. Countless times we return home for family celebrations and roles established many years earlier are reenacted. Thanksgiving and Christmas always bring about a series of bright red blushes as my family repeats youthful lapses. Work team members spend twenty years together, and still the image we have of them is the one created the first day that we meet.

Maybe because it is easier in the short term, we end up pigeonholing those around us. We create these single mental images and snapshots, freezing our frames. We manage by using outdated vignettes. We forget to revise and revalidate these beliefs. The experience and expertise gained during the ensuing decades are always tempered and overwhelmed by the early experience.

I am constantly astonished by the waste I see when this happens. Organizations spend millions of dollars each year to train their team members. Yet after the training, the team members return to "business as usual."

On the personal side, I want to grow old with my friends. I want to change and grow. I want them to change and grow. I want to listen to and laugh with them into my old age.

The process of creating our Centerlines makes us acknowledge those frozen images. We get a chance to break them and reframe.

Chapter 8

Within Our Own Centerline

"In other living creatures the ignorance of themselves is nature, but in man it is a vice."
- *Boethius*

A second insight came later that same cold, wintry afternoon. My niece had switched to another coloring book and was trying to connect the dots. As most of us do, she struggled to find the pattern, the right order in which to connect them. Also as most of us do, she decided to connect the dots in her own fashion and not in the fashion originally conceived.

Unlike what most of us face, in this instance there was a picture behind the dots. There was a concrete order to the dots. All the dots required were present.

Our world is not quite that simple. The order and purpose of our own dots, our own points, are not that simple to discern. I liken this to a three-dimensional image found within a fractal poster. Commonly found in the malls or along beachside boardwalks, these posters present a surface appearance of one image. Frequently this image is pretty innocuous, with mountains and streams and maybe some bouncing bunny rabbits.

However, if you look at it in another way you see a completely different image contained within it. Beneath the pastoral images are spaceships or Klingon warriors or other far-out images. You just have to look. I admit it; I generally can't see the images. I have to be in a highly relaxed state of mind to cut through the surface to see the pattern below. The harder I try, the less likely I am to see the image.

Our own life is like that. Surface images hide other meanings and insights. Images that lurk beneath our own surface need the right set of circumstances to spring forward. In the scheme of life, information is plentiful, and ideas are easy. Insights are what are truly difficult.

Remembering back to high school geometry, lines are composed of a connected infinite set of points on a single plane. Centerlines, like all lines, embody an infinite number of distinct points.

The "set points" are within us. We are composed of those that we are born with; we are composed of those that we discover; we are composed of those that we can change; and we are composed of those that cannot be changed. Our point sets have meaning both individually and as part of our grouped set.

As we seek to discover the meaning of our grouped set of points, our insights generally come in fits and starts, bits and pieces. Our revelations are normally fractal in nature. Each insight captures only a piece of what is being revealed. Our current perception and understanding tempers our discovery process. We realize that the underlying truth has many facets.

Further, our understanding of these truths is contextual. Our insights are part of a contextual, continual revelation process. Our revelations, although relational, are distinctly not relativistic in the philosophical sense, despite the fact that some would immediately suggest that. Our insights, even as they are based on the originator, the receiver, and the situation, struggle to recognize fundamental, transcendental truths.

Our fractal insights can be imagined as a series of internal and external points—grounding points, reference points, reflection points, pivot points, balance points. Connected, these points become the way an individual or organization looks at itself. They provide a rich technique that allows us to have the ability to reflect upon ourselves, our core, and our intent.

Chapter 9

Our Points Within

"To understand is to perceive patterns."
- *Isaiah Berlin*

I don't have fond memories of my high school geometry class. The topic was not one my strengths nor one of my interests. Still, some of the lessons learned follow me. The use of the set points as imagery for our own internal life resonates as a model.

Our mental set points are many, and some of the points noted earlier deserve elaboration. Obviously, the listed points are not exhaustive but merely illustrative.

- **Grounding points** are the basis by which we close our mental images. All around us are electrical outlets—some with two prongs; most with three. Years ago, engineers recognized that grounded electrical systems are inherently safer than ungrounded systems. The National Electrical Code defines a ground as: "a conducting connection, whether intentional or accidental, between an electrical circuit or equipment and the earth, or to some conducting body that serves in place of the earth." Just as electrical grounding points serve to complete the power loop, mental grounding points serve to complete our mental images.

- **Reference points** are external, "authoritative" sources that we cite to justify our beliefs and desires. Creeds and canons, financial statements and stock prices, technical guidelines and specifications—these are just some of the many reference points that we have.

- **Reflection points** are those items that we meditate on to find insights into our lives. Much in the way a piece of scripture forces us to sit back and reflect upon something, we all go through the process of reflecting upon those things that define us.

Our Centerlining process requires intentional reflection on a variety of things. You have to play "mental cat paws," looking at ideas and notions from various angles, and patting the reflections around mentally.

I characterize it as creating Koans for today, as we force a breakdown of our associative barriers. Much like our reactions when we break open fortune cookies and take fifteen seconds to joke about the contents, we can use the mundane to find fragments of understanding in everything.

Thinking about things such as the "smells" of music or the "colors" of scents allows us the liberty to find insights everywhere. We get to turn rocks over to see what else is there, and encourage our minds to view situations from completely new perspectives.

In addition to trying to see completely new perspectives, I love to learn from the personal insights and public writings of those who have gone before me. I confess to being a bit of a mental voyeur. I become totally absorbed in trying to see the perspectives found within historical journals.

My mind turns over its preexisting notions as I read the letters between Hannah Arendt and Mary McCarthy, or those between Rupert Brooke and James Strachey. I try to absorb the musings of Dag Hammarskjöld and relate his journey to my own. I peek into the diaries of Anaïs Nin in order to see how she was able to wrestle with her own insights.

I don't want to lose that past or to completely live in it. We think *for* ourselves, not *by* ourselves. We are the product of those who have gone before us, and not simply those whom we have met.

We should appreciate their insights, recognize where the insights came from, and reflect upon them. To paraphrase de Tocqueville, "(If) the past has ceased to throw its light onto the future, the mind of man will (cease)."

- **Pivot Points** are a way to see your Centerline from outside yourself. We all have those periods in our lives when we feel as though we are outsiders. If we are new to an area or a job, there is a temporary sense of not belonging. We all try to forget the awkward adolescent years during which we longed to fit in, never realizing that everyone else was feeling the same. If we can embrace the role of an outsider, our insights can be exceptionally liberating, for outsiders do have unique perspectives. You use these moments to take a chance to step outside your framework and pivot around your Centerline. In doing so, you gain different perspectives on your life.

For my second year of university, at the age of eighteen, I moved to Taiwan without possessing the ability to speak a word of Chinese. It was a radical immersion into a completely new culture. The transformative process of learning a new language and being given a new name, combined with a geographic isolation from family and friends, required me to pivot myself and adopt a dramatically different outlook.

There is a hazard in being an *Ausländer*. A systemic sense of being an outsider, based in such differences as racial, gender, religious, or sexual orientation, does lead to an endemic sense of alienation. I agree with Eric Hoffer, who, in *The True Believer*, wrote that a continual belief in being an *Ausländer* leads to a radical extremism, a desire for isolation, and an ill-founded sense of persecution. Our Centerlined journey will lead us along the path of inclusion through commonality.

- **Balance points** are those aspects in our life that help us as we constantly adjust ourselves. Both individual and organizational in nature, they can be the most difficult part of your Centerline to establish.

I constantly feel as though I am spinning plates or walking a tight wire as many competing factors seem to tug on my soul. I know that I'm not nearly as talented in my life as the performers in *Cirque du Soleil* are in theirs, and I have a continual fear that I will drop something. Yet I try to use my Centerline to balance my own life.

Individual balance points include where you focus your time: family, work, and church. An example of an organizational balance point is the niche in which an organization competes: price, service, or technology.

Each of our fractal insights goes through a Centerlining synthesis process. We unify this complex series of insights. With this process we actively choose and affirm the values by which we live. Our Centerline becomes part of our operating system.

We all struggle with where we find meaning, where we place value, and what we determine to be essential. When we reach an initial level of understanding, we are emboldened to explore the nuances found within our Centerline.

Again, using the aspects of your life from Chapters 3 and 4, think about the different "points" within them. What grounds them? What authoritative references do you use? How do you reflect upon them? How do you balance them in contrast and in support of other aspects of your life?

△1 △2 △3 △4

Grounding

Reference

Reflection

Balance

Other

       FIGURE 6: Your Points and Your Aspects

Chapter 10

Recognizing Our Own Centerline

"First, say to yourself what you would be; and then do what you have to do."
- Epictetus

Self-preservation, sex, money, power, pain, pleasure—these all are rather dark, Hobbesian, utilitarian views on life. To many, these are the very and only things that drive us. They are the attractions and attachments by which we allow ourselves to be defined. These attractions result in rather shallow, empty goals—goals that are ultimately unfulfilling.

We have our romantic side, our serious side, our tough side—sides that, if solely considered, present a skewed view. Still, it's not just work, it's not just others, it's not just religion, it's not just money that defines us. So what is it?

It is not just one single thing. It is all of these things and more and less and the way we put them together. We define and redefine ourselves constantly, and many elements contribute to our self-definition. We define ourselves by an additive process— the things that we pull towards us. We define ourselves by a subtractive process—the things that we push away from. We define ourselves by a connective process—the people and things that we link together. We define ourselves by our career, our role in society, our relationships, our offspring, and our affiliations.

For simplicity's sake, I use the model set forth by Shakti Gawain in *Creating True Prosperity* and group these elements into four categories: relationships, spiritual, physical, and career. I use the technique that we have gone through in the preceding chapters as I try to explore and understand each in depth, for each deserves extensive thought and contemplation. I've used my grounding, reference, reflection, pivot, and balance points as the basis to come to a greater understanding of these attributes. I would encourage you to look at those aspects you initially identified earlier in our journey and to see if you have elements in each of these categories.

I recognize that understanding these aspects is the first step of our journey. We still need to integrate them together, to find those things we hold in common with others, and then to establish ways to act.

Chapter 11

An Integrated Journey

> *"This is the journey that men make: to find themselves. If they fail in this it doesn't matter much what else they find."*
> - James Michener

Satisfied by the immediate, we routinely don't reflect on our real future. We center our debates on the "ethics" and "values" of the marketplace and do not nurture substantive values. We don't engage in the Centerlining process. Our emphasis on codified beliefs and material values causes us to lose sight of the essential nature of humankind.

We have to step away from the current overemphasis on either a mechanistic, materialistic world or a structured, closed, exclusive spirituality. This dualistic approach is particularly unhealthy, and our Centerlined journey traverses these two minefields. The journey requires a self-examination that can be intensely painful.

I've struggled to establish and link the elements of my own Centerline together in a meaningful way. I've filled whiteboards with my attempts to figure them out, and have scribbled on countless "Post-its"® to connect the different elements together.

This is a journey that has been related by mystics of many faith groups. The Christian mystic path, described by St. John of the Cross as the "Dark Night of Soul," is fraught with inner turmoil. Wonderfully described by Jim Marion in *Putting on the Mind of Christ,* the cycle of self-awareness brings us to depths of loneliness as well as to heights of insight as we move forward to realizing fully the inner Kingdom of God.

In Islam, the Sufis have a similar tradition. With seven phases in their devotional path, there is a progressive development and "unveiling of the heart." They struggle as they repeatedly surrender to God's love.

You don't have to do any of this. Frequently we step away from the abyss of the soul's dark night and we retreat to the comfort of a known safe place. In doing so, we may live, but not fully. We simply doodle.

Most of us rely on the immediate context rather than our Centerline to make routine decisions. For many of us, our actions take place without self-actualization and reflection, without our undergoing the transformative process to establish what it means to exist, really. Many go through life's drive-through, order the "Spiritual Happy Meal", and contentedly partake in McSpirituality.

Others pass by this drive-through to find a more nutritious meal. In the words of Kierkegaard's alter ego, Johannes Climacus, "But really to exist, so as to interpenetrate one's existence with consciousness, at one and the same time eternal and as if we are removed from existence, and yet also present in existence and in the process of becoming: that is truly difficult."

So, what is the real cost of doing nothing? What is the cost to us? What is the cost for not recognizing and helping others through their journey?

Chapter 12

Seeing Other Centerlines

"Hear the other side."
- Saint Augustine

How many times do we drive along and get frustrated as the driver next to us "intentionally" cuts us off or switches lanes to "get ahead" of us? Why can't other people see how important something really is? Why do we personalize each of these encounters and think that it is "all about me"? Why do we have this inclination to believe that the small part of the world that we live in is the center of the entire world?

As we develop our own Centerline, to be complete we must realize that all the people around us also have their own Centerline, the way in which they have framed their own decisions and beliefs. We need to see the drawings within their doodles.

Born in South Carolina and growing up in Connecticut, I listened to my southern and Yankee friends. Attending university in Indiana, I listened to my friends from the heartland. I listened to a wonderful Muslim girl in Singapore describe her religion to me. I listened to the Romanian family describe their lives while traveling with them on the Trans-Siberian railroad. I listened to my North Carolina friends whom I met in Korea, lived with in Georgia, and had dinner with while they were working in Switzerland. I listened to the open source software developers and the data jocks at the Jet Propulsion Laboratory.

For all of their incredible diversity, almost all of them had similar dreams and goals; almost all of them wanted similar things for their families and friends. We all shared a fundamental similarity; we had many points of commonality. We knew that we all had gifts that we wanted to embrace, to relish, and to share. We all had potential. We all knew that others had gifts that they wanted to embrace, to relish, and to share. We knew that the others had potential that we wanted them to fulfill.

We wanted to recognize our points of commonality. We wanted to bring our own understanding and gifts to each other. We knew that the more developed each of our Centerlines are, the more unified we all are in both thought and action.

We should stop to think about what works for whom and in what circumstances. For example, we determine what types of medication are good for preschoolers, but these differ from those that are appropriate for young adults. Treatments differ between the middle aged and the elderly. As we Centerline, we find a way to give these same nuanced answers in all of life.

Clearly, our Centerlines never totally overlap, for we can never all see things in exactly the same way. The more developed they are, the more we synchronize our family, our friends, our community, and our organizations. The things that we hold in common pull us all together. We recognize the legitimacy of other perspectives.

An interesting exercise in this process is to have a spouse, partner, or friend draw a values diagram similar to the one you did in Chapter 3. Compare your results. You can clearly see what you hold in common and where you differ.

Chapter 13

Commonality

"We were born to unite with our fellow men, and to join in community with the human race."
- Cicero

A crucial step in Centerlining is recognizing our points of commonality. We empirically know that over 98% of our DNA is the same as everyone else's. Statistically it is possible that we all have breathed not only the same air, but the same air as Abraham, Jesus, Mohammad, Genghis Khan, Hitler, and Stalin. We don't emotionally acknowledge nor intellectually embrace that. We focus on our individuality rather than our sense of community. We have not focused on finding our commonalities.

We have focused on exploring ourselves. Books on finding ourselves abound. Pop psychology lets us all find our inner child. We have focused on discovering the "natural" laws. Scientific and pseudo-scientific treatises surround us.

There is a nascent trend to find ways to connect. With a focus toward the business world, bestsellers such as *The Medici Effect* and programs such as the PBS/Learning Channel show "Connections" stress the benefits found by connecting seemingly random events and inventions. In the world of science, string theory seeks to establish a grand, scientific-based theory of unification. Brilliant minds have spent many days and dollars thinking about these things.

In our own fashion, we can do the same. Centerlining helps us intentionally seek and establish commonality. We can identify, and should strengthen, the linkages of those things that we have in common. The merchant and scientific states are important; our state of self is important; our interconnected state is as important.

This discussion is grounded in the writings of Karl Popper, Jürgen Habermas, and Ken Wilber. They outline three components in our view of the world:

- **I** – Subjective, self-consciousness, self-expression, ego

- **It** – Objective, science and technology, empirical forms, universal truths

- **We** – Commonality, worldviews, common context, mutual understanding

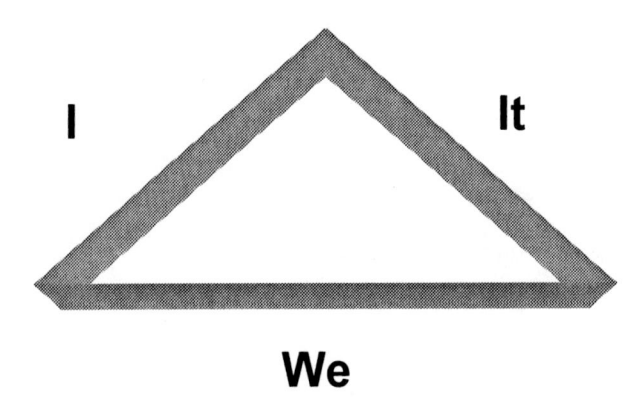

FIGURE 7: Worldview Triangle

We have learned to differentiate between the three; we have gained an understanding of the "I" and the "It." We have not learned how to allow development of the "We." We have not learned how to integrate the three. Much like a stool that requires three solid and uniform legs to be stable, our society needs three legs.

This is one of our tasks within Centerlining: to develop the third leg and to integrate it. We have to invest time and effort in our social infrastructure, in our "we."

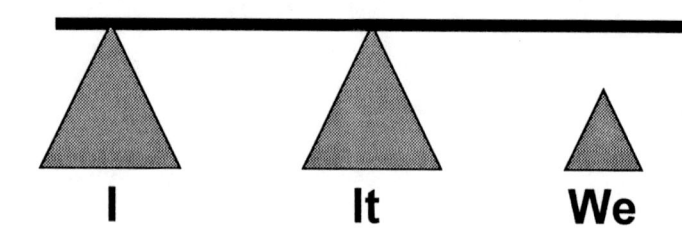

FIGURE 8: Balancing Our Worldview's Legs

How do we find ways to connect to everyone? We all seek to find points on which we can agree with others. Our socialization process naturally demands that we do so. We each possess a social nature that calls us to seek things that we can relate to ourselves and in turn relate to each other. Current cultural artifacts of this tendency include the parlor game of finding six degrees of separation and subscribing to the "Friendster" Web site.

It is a struggle and it is tough not to become cynical or jaded in the process. My own search for commonality has been a long one and, at times, I think that I've stretched the boundaries a bit. My undergraduate essay, in retrospect, overreached as I tried to cross-analyze three very distinct schools of philosophy—classical Taoism, the German idealism of Georg Hegel, and the French phenomenalism of writer Maurice Merleau-Ponty. Although the common strains of thought were there, my particular analysis suffered from a lack of perspective.

My master's essay used chaos theory as an organizing tool for complex information technology systems. But chaos theory, as opposed to string theory, let me create patterns from the tops of the waves rather than from the currents underneath the water. As do so many, I keep looking for ways to connect the dots and see a whole pattern within a daily life.

And as so many do, I can confuse mere coincidence with causality or actuality. Finding true commonality means finding that actuality. Our Centerlining helps us relate it all together.

Chapter 14

Searching For Commonality

"When men understand what each other means they see, for the most part, that controversy is either superfluous or hopeless."
- *John Henry Cardinal Newman*

So, how do we find ways to find a connection, a linkage, with each and every person we meet in a given day? How do we make purposeful efforts to find these combinations? How do we avoid false or superficial points of commonality?

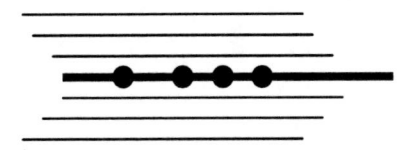

As we consciously reflect, we start our self-definition process. We make visible those things that we deem important.

Figure 9: Points on Our Centerline

As we better define ourselves, we see points of commonality with others and the things that they deem important.

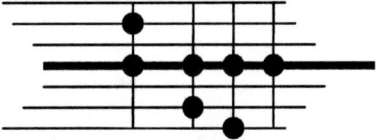

Figure 10: Common Points Across Centerlines

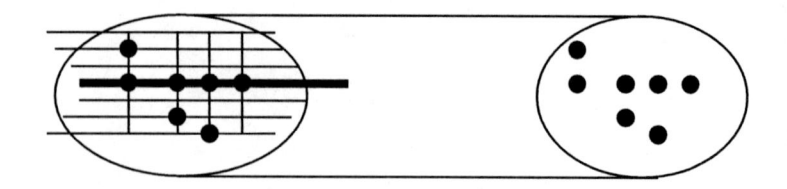

Figure 11: Recognizing Other Points

We can see the differences along the Centerlines and can still find common ground. This common ground gives us the ability to give rights to different views and create a truly civil society.

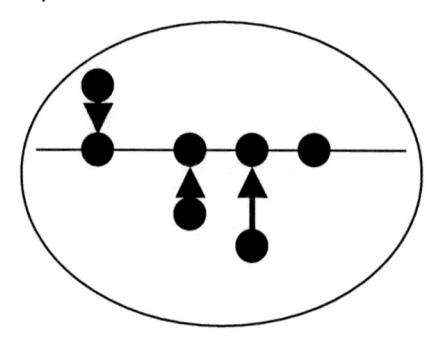

Figure 12: Finding Commonality

The current focus on the development of a techno/egotistical culture and not on a contemplative/connected culture has given us a superficial style and method. It has not given us the substantive one that we all long for.

Our task is to create an environment that allows us at least to understand each other and find our commonality. Our journey starts as we recognize our Centerlines, while also beginning to recognize the Centerlines of others. The result is unity, but not uniformity.

Chapter 15

Finding Commonality

"God creates men, but they choose each other."
- Niccolò Machiavelli

We expend an amazing amount of effort searching for relationships, yet we frequently don't realize that each encounter can be one in which we recognize a kindred spirit. We don't recognize our fundamental similarities.

We have all played the "connect the dot" game at cocktail parties. This is when we try to figure out where we know someone from. We try to talk about something of mutual interest—why we are at the event or our reaction to the food. With a small or similar effort, we should be able to find some trait in common with each person that we meet. We can look anyone in the eye and find something in common.

The basics of socializing fill the shelves in countless libraries. There is an industry based on teaching us the art of influencing people and winning friends. Techniques abound on how best to find a way to connect with people to extract something from them.

Centerlining helps identify those things that we truly hold in common—values, beliefs, goals, dreams. Centerlining doesn't make these connections visible as a way to manipulate. Rather, we create and nurture our points of commonality to encourage and support others.

Chapter 16

Common Places

> *"We have to develop stable popular organizations, and a culture of concern, and commitment, and activism, and solidarity, which can help to sustain us in these struggles and which can help break down some of the barriers that have been set up to divide and distract us."*
> - *Noam Chomsky*

The ongoing recreation of "Third Places" is emblematic of this search for commonality. A "Third Place" is our local coffee house, Irish pub, Asian teahouse, or Middle Eastern hookah. These are the places where we can share a cup of coffee or pint of beer. These places make all the difference, for they give us a place to pause as we discover ourselves and others. We saw this in the intellectual ferment of the sixteenth- and seventeenth-century English teahouses; we saw this in the coffee shops of eighteenth-century Paris; we are starting to see this today in our new Third Places.

These Third Place providers create a place to nurture our sense of self, of others, and of wonder. These shops foster a space to savor nuanced varietals of beverage and self as they create a new public space open to anyone. Where there was previously none, there is a new common meeting spot.

My family and friends love to meet in these spots—to connect with old friends, meet new friends, hold meetings, sit and think, or surf the Internet. It is amazing how open we are in our Third Places. As we take the time and sip that cup, we relax, open up, and reflect. We allow a different, more nuanced sense of self to emerge. For every action, like each cup of coffee, holds a promise, a promise that a small action or sip can transform our day and our lives.

These places and our reflections create environments that foster commonality. It is commonality that helps to overcome our individual, societal, and ethical egotism, that sense of self-absorption that dominates most of our lives. The establishment of a Centerline helps us resolve the discontinuities within ourselves and among others.

Chapter 17

Challenges to Commonality

"We choose our joys and sorrow long before we experience them."
- Kahlil Gibran

In our search for commonality, we find a great deal of resistance. There are those who benefit by the divisiveness and others who simply find this search to be naïve.

Our hyper-politically charged world has numerous "factions" that pollute the atmosphere by generating wedge issues. We become polarized and isolated by those who intentionally spread discord. We grow to see life in a completely adversarial light.

I'm saddened as I listen to hate radio and television. These pundits offer only the basest, most unrefined opinions. They have hijacked the polity as they play to the lowest common denominators and to our fears. They offer up belligerent bravado as well-principled discourse. They are dangerous, as they poison society by their faulty logic, incivility, and bile.

Assuredly, most of us do not consider such antics "normal discourse." We see them as the menace they are and we need to call them to account. We just can't let them continue to have such a strong influence.

Their political discourse takes the easy way out by creating and nurturing differences. Politics should not be a dirty word; politics is merely a form of social interaction. There is no "them" or "us." Government is one actualization of our sense of "we."

Similarly, there are those who would find this entire discussion to be completely simplistic and unrealistic. There is a measure of truth to that. During dinner at a recent conference on terrorism, I was describing

Centerlining in general terms. Some dinner companions were intrigued; others immediately dismissed me as a sunny optimist. It was easy for them to give in to a disdainful, negative outlook. But, when you do the right thing, and assert your humanity and Centerline, you can start to change at least your small part of the world.

Chapter 18

Reflection, Not Obsession

"There is only one meaning of life: the act of living itself."

- Erich Fromm

Although Centerlining requires a process of reflection, it also demands action. Analysis paralysis is endemic within most organizations. We somehow have come to believe in the inherent value of navel gazing. We calculate the compound interest value of accumulated belly button lint.

While we reflect to find our Centerline, we cannot simply remove ourselves from society and concentrate on finding a sense of inner well-being. We have to step away from the trap that Herman Hesse laid out in *The Glass Bead Game*.

Hesse's novel discussed a closed society that valued mental activity to the exclusion of virtually anything else. With high barriers between the physical and mental worlds, the leading character had to come to a point of decision. He needed to step away from his particular society and back into the world as a whole. His intellectual ghetto was an inviting and comforting place, but it was still a ghetto.

And we each have our own particular ghetto, where we live in a false sense of security. We can't get caught into our own Glass Bead trap; we must not recoil from the whole of society.

I've continued to cultivate depth of understanding in all aspects of my life. I have come to appreciate, almost to the point of obsession, wine. Beginning with extremely straightforward boxed wines in college and moving to more complex variations, I happily embrace the idea that life is too short to drink bad wine. I have spent hours searching for the right combination to go with a certain dish. I took an eight-week Wine Captains course to understand better what I was doing. I replaced all my stemware with glasses specifically designed to enhance particular varietals. I consult with my local wine merchant or one of my wine distributors to find the right bottles. I renovated one of the rooms in my home and built a full wine cellar so I could properly cellar bottles for an extended period of time.

This significant effort was undertaken so I could understand and appreciate the wine's frame—its nuances, its flavors, and its textures. It allowed me to reflect fully on the qualities of the wine that I shared with friends and family. I never lost sight of the fact that the wine was meant to be enjoyed. It had no real value outside the enjoyment it would bring to me and others. My efforts were designed to let us live in the wine's moment, and they serve as models for my own daily activities.

This same obsessive effort needs to be applied to understanding our own and others' frames and Centerlines. We have to live in each and every moment. As each moment goes by, we should contemplate it, and embrace it. In the Buddhist sense, we are called to embrace and be mindful of each moment.

Being actively mindful is just one aspect of our lives; we are called to live in this world. We are called to act. As with the blank piece of paper that my niece used to frame her artistic creation, we reflect and act in order to create our Centerline.

Chapter 19

Activity vs. Action

"Action indeed is the sole medium of expression of ethics."
- Jane Addams

In much the same way that we have a tendency to obsess about the smallest of details rather than reflect about the real issues, we also have a tendency to confuse activity for meaningful action. We let routine activity—taking out the trash, putting away the dishes—consume the entirety of our daily lives. We think that our doodles are finished masterpieces.

For centuries, most of us were rightly focused on the day-to-day tasks needed to survive. In our time and place, these basics are, or should be, readily available. We get to worry about what type of cereal to eat in the morning, not whether there will be food available. We wait for the shower water to warm up, not walk miles to haul the water home.

We use activity as a way of avoiding ourselves, substituting activity for awareness. There is a rampant, mistaken belief that this activity equals progress. We falsely assume that the more we act, the more we are alive. We fill ourselves with empty, fast food–like activity. It's easy to open up the bag of salt-laden chips and turn on a television or play a video game. We confuse our focus on minutia for meaningful action.

Action is purpose-driven behavior leading to long-term value. Striking items off the "To Do" list does not amount to accomplishing your goals or creating true value. Projects that are on time and on budget but never get customer acceptance are useless activities. We need to take the time to ensure that the effort and resources expended really contribute to our long-term goals.

We have to get off our fast-food diet. Life, like the grocery store, gives us a huge variety of options. We have to take the time and effort to have a nutritious diet. Centerlining helps us read the labels on the food and helps us ensure that we practice reflective, purposeful action.

Chapter 20

Risk

"Life is 'trying things to see if they work.'"
- Ray Bradbury

Our call to action is also a call to embrace risk. Risk is both exhilarating and frightening. Risk is passion-driven. Risk is an external force. Risk is an internal turmoil.

Risk can be liberating. I've assisted at one of the local cooking schools and am continually on the lookout for new foods and techniques. There is a challenge in combining flavors and textures, timing the preparation, and finding the right complements with courses. You have to dig into the endeavor and play with the food. As one of my instructors nicely put it, "Cooking is a contact sport." Sometimes it works, sometimes it doesn't, and sometimes you call the pizza delivery service.

Our lives are the same. Sometimes they work; sometimes they don't; sometimes we call for carryout. But when we take risks, we leave ourselves open to the process of continual discovery and revelation. By grounding risk taking in your Centerline, you can pick something important and take the chance to grow. Taking the chance to be original or creative is risky, but it is the mark of Centerlined action.

Chapter 21

Fear

"Fear is not the natural state of civilized people."
- *Aung San Suu Kyi*

Realizing that our acceptance of risk is necessary to Centerline, the development of our ability to overcome our fears is also necessary. Trying or learning something new is very uncomfortable. Our creativity is a raw, unbridled emotion. Establishing, integrating, and living one's Centerline makes not only ourselves but also those around us very uncomfortable.

How does one get over this discomfort, these fears? Can we ever? Should we? Or do we find ways to cope with them? Many of our worst fears have been with us since childhood. Our age and maturity do not necessarily enable us to cope with them. In fact, our coping mechanisms routinely gloss over the underlying cause of the fear.

Our fears fall into some broad categories: fear of losing control of our urges, feelings, and rational thoughts; fear of losing the love of others and the love of ourselves; fear of appearing weak or foolish; fear of damage to our bodies; fear of our own death and the death of those near to us; and fear of losing order and structure in our world.

We each have our own particular set of insecurities and fears. I know that I don't like feeling inadequate. I really dislike not being able to fix all the problems that get tossed my way. It does not matter how inconsequential my fear might seem to others; it is very real to me. But my fear may be grounded in unrealistic expectations and my inability to let go and trust.

But by letting go, we end up becoming stronger. We learn to trust others; we learn to let them help us. In the aftermath of one of the natural disasters that routinely hit the southern part of the United States, I received an e-mail from a friend. In it he did one of the bravest things imaginable: he asked for help. I turned over all night as I visualized the images of complete and total devastation that he related. He described the lake rising, and the water overwhelming his family. In the course of a few short hours, everything was gone. They managed to survive by escaping in an old, clunkering truck. And it was not just his immediate family that was impacted, but his entire extended family. Their entire support structure was wiped away. For the first time, his tight-knit, self-sufficient Cajun family had to look beyond its ties of blood kin for assistance. He expressed his embarrassment about asking for help; he expressed his embarrassment for being embarrassed. He was brave and let go of his fear to ask. He learned to trust us more, and we came to learn more about him. And we all gained a greater love and respect for each other.

By not letting go, we can be manipulated by our fears. Society is grounded in fear. It is so entrenched that we don't know what it feels like to live without fear surrounding us—our fear of terrorism, our fear of weapons of mass destruction, our fear of poverty, our fear of failure, our fear of poor health.

Further, we have those who foster fear. Politicians lead us down frightful paths. The media shows us only the "fires and crimes" of the day. Their manipulation lets them drive us in their desired direction. We get accustomed to living in a perpetual state of fear and build walls to protect ourselves.

How do we break down these walls? What techniques do you use to remove fear in your own and others' lives? When we come to the understanding of self and others found from Centerlining, we can achieve the crucial step of acknowledging, communicating, and overcoming our fears. Further, we can stand ready to help others overcome their fears as well.

Chapter 22

Translucence

"Life is a luminous halo, a semi-transparent envelope surrounding us from the beginning."
- Virginia Woolf

As we seek to find ways to live our Centerline, we daily shake our heads upon hearing the doublespeak endemic within society.

Overtly addressing a particular problem, the true intent of the speaker is something very different. Nothing frustrates us more as we shake our heads and think, "Why don't you just say what you really mean?" We know that this is wrong.

We need transparency, for by bringing in light and perspective we can prevent fraud, short-circuit greed, and avoid stupidity. Truth does not suffer in the light. But our transparency needs to be nuanced. There is a right to privacy, and some matters are exceptionally sensitive—just because you can say something doesn't mean you should.

We have all sat in too many meetings where managers and leaders presented only a single side of a story. They knowingly skewed a presentation or series of "facts" as they spun their story. I had one boss who routinely berated my ability to manage the telephone services for his multimillion-dollar, privately held company. He screamed, he yelled, he turned a particularly interesting shade of lavender. He wanted costs reduced and he wanted services improved. He wanted a lot. But, every time I suggested that we switch our service provider or at least formally explore other options, he found reasons to put off the decision. He never found a reason to put off the degrading behavior. He never seemed to want to change our vendor; he actually seemed to prefer to rant and rave. However, his silent ownership of a significant percentage of that other company may have also had something to do with his indecision. His real agenda was not on the table. There was neither transparency nor translucence.

Centerlining fosters clarity. By understanding ourselves and our motives, we can better understand what and how to present ourselves to others. Our agendas and perspectives become explicit, balanced, and justified. We say what we really mean.

The critical reasoning behind the Centerlined process brings a high level of intellectual honesty to the game. We clean out the debris of the past and give ourselves and others the ability to let go and move on.

This type of break is not easily accomplished. We are raised with the impulse to hide our shortcomings and faults; we build our lives around structures of deceit that we believe to be inescapable.

The creation of a well-reasoned, candid environment is difficult. We need to have observers as brutally honest *and* universally respected as Lord Acton to cut through the "Alice in Wonderland" logic that permeates society.

The Centerlined value of simply telling the truth is fundamental. Our approach is not taken with minimalist constraints or concentrated on legalistic attributes. Honesty is maximalist. We should strive to live *in* the truth.

Our fidelity is not to the mere meanings of the words but to our actual intentions. Honesty is grounded in the behavior characteristics of commission and omission. We need to ensure that we *don't commit* improper acts and we need to ensure that we *don't omit* doing proper acts.

Concurrently, confessional television notwithstanding, we don't need to know all the details of everyone's life. As a Chinese expression goes, each family has books from which we should not read aloud. The drama of full disclosure is not necessarily appropriate. The shift in perspective is that we want to have a translucent quality to our lives—not total transparency.

Transparency is the complete exposure of all aspects—every detail is out for public display and review. Oprah has booked us for a week and Larry King is on hold. Translucence is partial opacity, a nuanced approach to self-exposure. Centerlining finds the appropriate balance in what to disclose and what not to disclose.

As one who has worked within classified environments, I understand the need for confidentiality. But as both an original member of the U.S. Central Command's detainee abuse investigation team and the founder of a company focused on the whistleblower provisions of Sarbanes-Oxley, I have struggled with finding the balance point between complete disclosure and complete secrecy.

As the supervisor of the U.S. Central Command's Records Management and Freedom of Information Act team, I was amazed at the increase in classification activity. I do not mean to imply anything nefarious. It simply seemed that trivial records are withdrawn and access barriers are increased reportedly in the interests of national security. Maybe what is actually being protected is simply inconvenient or embarrassing? As I noted earlier, truth does not suffer in the light.

The translucent quality of a Centerlined approach is my solution. Once again, as the Chinese expression goes, each family has books from which we should not read aloud. We need to know on which shelf the important books are. We do need to check them out, to read them to ourselves, and maybe, just maybe, to share.

Chapter 23

Grounding Our Centerline

> *"Religion is to do right. It is to love, it is to serve, it is to think, it is to be humble."*
> - *Ralph Waldo Emerson*

The attempts to impose a strict codification of particular viewpoints have been the cause of much strife and bloodshed over the centuries. The conflicts between three of the major faith groups—Islam, Judaism, and Christianity—are constantly in the spotlight. Yet they all began and have derived inspiration from a single font. Their font is found within the prophet Abraham.

According to the philosopher Bertrand Russell, all religions start with a blasphemy, a radical departure from beliefs long held and widely considered sacred and true. Abraham was such a blasphemer. His was a world of multiple gods who divided and conquered, but our fundamental unity was a truth that had to be spoken.

As we focus on the unifying nature of this founder, we see that Abraham had a very clear, compelling Centerline. He broke through his tradition and recognized the compelling, true nature of a monotheistic religion, a belief in a single God. He had a belief in a single God who is both nameless and unknowable. But, in what may be a revisionist interpretation, his belief was also a belief in a single, unifying God who is approachable and loving.

For God is not tribal; God is communal. God is not exclusive; God is inclusive. This insight was found before the journey in the wilderness, before the Cross, and before the trek to Medina. God was found before religions had to govern.

Fully explored, Abraham's Centerline allows one to see within others the same core value—love—that we should see in ourselves. In a seemingly radical but strikingly simple approach, this insight is the one that prophets through all times have tried to impart to their followers.

As did the others who came after him, Abraham struggled to have his revelation accepted. His revelation was one of many on the path of continual revelations that we are still called to listen to.

We can all sense and understand this presence and these revelations. I vividly recall the moments when I truly felt the grace of God—when friends were prostrate in front of an altar as they took their final vows for the priesthood, or I was praying next to my father's bed as he passed away. There was the tingling sensation of mystical grace within those rooms at those moments.

I also vividly recall the time in my life when I intellectually recognized the fundamental similarities of the major faith groups. I was on holiday in southeast Asia. Traveling on my own, with backpack and limited resources, I started the trip in Hong Kong at the Maryknoll House in Stanley. I spent days in Bangkok teaching English at one of the largest Buddhist temples in the world. I accompanied Hindu pilgrims in Malaysia to shrines within caves, and ended the trip touring Singapore with a Muslim. I was aware that these seemingly different groups of believers approached the same God but approached God from very dissimilar frameworks.

Our Centerline should foster similar understandings and expressions of faith and love. With profound differences in emphasis and approach, it is difficult to realize the single focus found within these faith groups. Many would contend that finding similarities among the many faiths is simply superficial, if not heretical. Yet a close examination of them and their original intent reveals commonality. I contend that stressing the differences is in itself a form of heresy.

It is not only the canons of Muhammad and Christ that make daily life sacred. Ideas alone do not make a religion survive. Equally important are the social and political structures that unite people. Our actions need to encourage our spiritual commonality. From sacramental rituals such as baptism and confirmation, to the "Liturgy of the Hours" and calls to pray, to devotions and the hajj, successful organized religions have not only compelling ideas but also compelling actions. Highly effective and organized religious systems, such as the Catholic Church, externally express unified Centerlines. Our Centerlines encompass not only the texts of our canons but also the natural rhymes of daily life.

As a caveat, it is also false to think that all positions are equally correct. It would be wonderful to say that after we genuinely understand someone, all significant disagreements disappear. That is simply not the case. There are transcendental truths, and Centerlining allows us to discover our approach to these truths.

Chapter 24

Continual Revelations

> *"To exist is to change, to change is to mature, to mature is to go on creating oneself endlessly."*
> - *Henri Bergson*

In any time of transition, we all feel the anxiety of the modernizing process. We feel tension. Our tension is natural, for it is a tension based in our struggle to find our Centerlines.

The change of pace in society and within individuals does not mirror the pace of change within technology. We know and feel that the pace of new technology continues to increase. We readily see the digitalization of the world, the introduction of nanotechnologies, and the progress in string theory. If, in the past, we found it difficult to reconcile the external and internal, then we should realize that the future will be even more difficult to comprehend.

Disruptive innovations continually unsettle the carts of tradition. Many have seen the process of modernity as an assault on tradition and values. Plato's telling account of the death of Socrates for his "corrupting" influence is just one example of many, and historical journals are replete with the similar anguish of elders and guardians of tradition as they try to push back this tide.

To overcome this tension and try to make sense of it all, we frequently turn to familiar, comforting frameworks. We crave a secure sense of self, a truth upon which we can absolutely depend. We seek to find the "right answer."

We turn to well-developed, concrete, codified expressions and frameworks. Our inability to tolerate ambiguity in the face of enormously complicated problems leads us to an almost automatic acceptance of structure and form, even if that structure and form are immature.

In bringing our commonality forward, we see the struggle between the continual process of revelation and static, brittle, closed ontological frameworks. How do we encourage a continual process of revelation?

A society based solely on the Koran cannot cite a verse for a parking ticket. We can't find a reference to M-theory in Revelations. Although doing so might be easier than the alternative, we can't selectively concentrate on particular pieces of a canon while neglecting the pieces that don't fit our particular purpose. We have to be honest enough to assess our canons critically in their entirety and understand their context.

I am more than a bit envious of believers who confess with absolute certainty and self-righteousness. I wish that I had the confidence to say with absolute certainty that I know exactly what God wants. I don't. I am comfortable with not knowing and with simply trusting.

The anger, rage, and bitterness from the advocates of their particular, absolute positions are neither illuminating nor informative. The idea that there is a single correct way to live is delusional and filled with an unseemly arrogance. Sadly, such advocates condemn the questioning, using the questioning as the basis for accusations of idolatry.

Ironically, the true problem resides in our failure to question, to embrace the unknowable, to accept the gifts of the changing world. We have an obligation to use our gifts and question. Those who would force their closed, brittle positions upon us are engaging in a spiritual hijacking.

Chapter 25

False Surety

> *"Doubt is not a pleasant condition, but certainty is absurd."*
> - Voltaire

Still, why do these closed ontological frameworks have such a broad appeal? They appeal for exclusivity—"only by being one of us can you be saved"—and they appeal to fear—"join us or be condemned." They also appeal to our tendency to take the path of least resistance and give in to an ease of understanding.

The more closed a doctrine is, the less it requires deep thinking. Highly simplified truths and slogans seem to explain everything. Our beliefs are condensed to bumper stickers and ten-second sound bites; our religious practices are streamlined to mere checklists.

This idolatry of surety allows people to worship the structure and beliefs of the "known" and absolute, rather than have faith in the unknown as we love and connect with each other. As the Gospel of Matthew notes, man is judged not on his adherence to orthodoxy but how he deals with the "hungry, the thirsty, the stranger, the naked, the sick, the disposed and the imprisoned." As we mature and overcome our fears, we can accept the continuing revelation process and the risks associated with the changes brought forth by these revelations.

Growing up, I didn't quite understand that some scripture was intentionally excluded from the Christian Bible. As a child, I thought that it contained everything about that time and place. As a young adult, I came to realize that inclusion was not automatic and that early church councils determined a large amount of the content.

The discovery of the Dead Sea Scrolls dramatically changed our understanding of early Christian history. The scrolls describe numerous strains of early Christian belief and many different versions of orthodoxy. More than one scholar has publicly stated that the scrolls should never have been found; many religious leaders have tried to wish their existence away.

The scrolls uprooted the previously accepted "truth" of a single, cohesive, unified early Christian community. These scriptures provide a fascinating insight into the early Christian communities, showing multiple forms of early Christian teaching. The sheer amount of diversity causes extreme unease to those who would contend, in an airbrushing of history, that there was a golden time of uniform unity.

Further, the struggle to grasp the continuing revelation was not limited only to these early Christian communities or even to Christians exclusively. Throughout Western history we see how varying beliefs about the nature and practice of religion create societal conflicts. The Reformation and Counter-Reformation, Vatican II and subsequent re-entrenchment of the Catholic Church, and numerous other examples show that attempts to restrict the expression of faith to a set, single fashion have either caused turmoil and bloodshed or have made the faith irrelevant.

Other Abrahamic faiths saw a similar early outpouring of inquiry and tension. In the "Golden" Era of Islam, there was an established process by which each facet of belief was critically examined—the notion of an Ijtihad. Traditionally, Ijtihad is defined as the Islamic tradition of independent inquiry by Islamic legal scholars. It called for a spirit of critical inquiry to examine Islamic scriptures and practices. There are historical and contemporary scholars, such as Mohammed Arkoun, who hold that the practice of Ijtihad can be done by all followers of Islam.

While military threats and economic shifts of that era may have been some of the underlying factors, it appears that the practice of Ijtihad was discouraged and relegated to history in an attempt to ensure unity within the Muslim sphere. In short, the practice of Ijtihad did not endure. In a process not dissimilar from the creation of a single creed in the early Christian communities, Islamic scholars froze debate within Islam. All answers were in place; the

Shariah provided a fixed blueprint for society. Critical reasoning was no longer desirable. Instead, the answers lay in the past and in the rulings of the established canon.

Today, this debate remains frozen, and advocates of critical inquiry are vilified. Still, the tradition of Ijtihad exists and it gives Muslims the ability to update calcified religious practices in light of contemporary circumstances.

I want to understand better the origins of our belief systems, the situation in which these early prophets expressed their message and the way their followers tried to synthesize their fractal experience with the transcendental. I want a trip to the Middle East to explore where Jesus spent his youth, where Mohammad honeymooned. I want to walk the land in the same fashion as the Buddha, and spend nights under the stars like the Sufi. I want to know what buffeted them, what questions they asked, and what led them to their particular expressions of understanding. I would like to experience why something was thought and understood.

When any of us converts our values into a rote and calcified ideology, we inevitably simplify its spiritual potential. We cut out its heart; we make it brittle; we limit its love. There are complexities, ambiguities, and contradictions in the world and in our struggle. This streamlined and simplified approach dams the deep river of love, turning it into a shallow, silted creek. But as we Centerline, we cross over this dam to a deeper, albeit more complicated life—a life that is Centerlined in love.

Chapter 26

Centerlining Love

> *"Your task is not to seek for love, but merely to seek and find all the barriers within yourself that you have built against it."*
>
> *- Rumi*

Thomas Jefferson's classic re-editing of the Bible sought to find the "true" words of Jesus of Nazareth and his transcendental message, with a resulting emphasis, not on miracles, but rather on what has been termed the 11th commandment—Love Your Neighbor as Yourself. The mystics of the early Church Fathers, the Sufi, the Kabbalists, and the Dead Sea Gospels all focus on this overwhelming, elusive concept of love. Centerlining focuses on this love—love for self, love for others, love for God.

As human emotion, love is perhaps the most talked about aspect of life. Yet it is the least understood aspect of human life. Every individual experiences love in an absolutely unique manner.

Over the course of many centuries, many brilliant theologians and philosophers have attempted to describe and categorize the wonder and depth of this emotion. Efforts to find a universal meaning invariably lead to a vast oversimplification. Categories large enough to contain the vastness but deep enough to capture the nuances have proven exceptionally difficult to find. The ancient Greeks put forward three commonly recognized aspects of love that seem to articulate all of these nuances best:

- **Phileo:** Friendship, strengthened by shared experiences

- **Eros:** Sensual love, stimulated by our senses

- **Agape**: Pure love, selflessly and unconditionally expressed

Phileo   **Eros**

Love

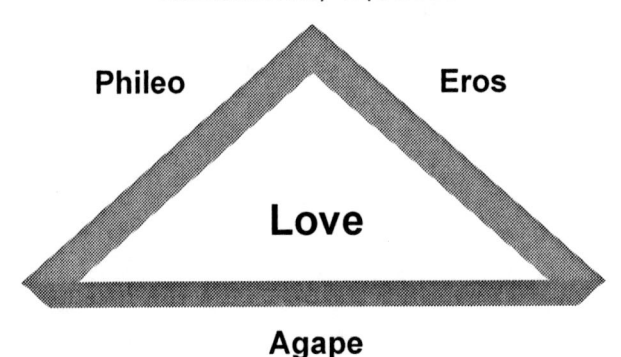

Agape

FIGURE 13: Aspects of Love

Unfortunately, in our unreflective society, most of us have accepted a pretty low common denominator for love, almost to the point of love's becoming a vulgar commodity. We essentially think that love is a mixture between being popular (*phileo*) and having sex appeal (*eros*).

We have ignored the *agape*, the sense of selfless love. We have narrowed our search to finding ways of being loved rather than of developing our capacity to love. We have come to think of the limited commodities of popularity and sex appeal as the limits of love. Real love, much like Divine Grace, has no limits. It is not a bounded commodity; there is an endless supply.

Accepting this pure love is a choice. We choose to be open to it, accept it, and give it. Pure love is active, not passive. It is giving, not receiving. Pure love breaks through our walls of isolation and emptiness. It is a unity that allows us to be ourselves and to retain our integrity. It enables us to accept our differences within relationships and to choose to love the person. Like finding commonality, our expression of pure love takes effort.

Our journey is on a road graded with pure love. Life within a realized state of love helps make external "the kingdom of heaven" that Jesus and other founding prophets talked about being "within you." Like our recognition of our sense of "we," acknowledging and fostering the *agape* leads to a sense of self-respect and respect for others, and an environment conducive to the Centerlining of love. This acknowledgement and Centerlining demands a high level of intimacy and trust, for it lets others see you as you really are, and lets you see others as they really are.

Chapter 27

Centerline Rules?

"My doctrine is not a doctrine but just a vision. I have not given you any set of rules. I have not given you a system."
- *Siddhartha Gautama*

Our journey would be much simpler if the rules found in the virtual gaming world were the ones found in the real world. In the gaming world, we are the hero, boss, star; there is always an answer; the world has a logical basis; relationships are structured.

In the gaming world, there is determinism and we have no absolute, real choice. This world and our role within it are already completely constructed. Everything is logical and knowable.

Real life isn't a question of inputs and outputs, of spending X amount of time to get Y results; there is no spreadsheet that allows you to program life or love. Our Centerline has to be aware of this uncertainty.

Although the real world is already constituted, it is never completely constructed. A man is acted upon and acts upon; he acts within himself and within others. There is never complete determinism and never absolute choice. Man is never merely a thing and never merely a bare consciousness. We get to choose; we get to draw.

The world of predetermined outcomes is wonderfully, if superficially, self-affirming. The world of choice is scary. We fear risk; we fear failure; we fear the unknown. As we find out during our discovery of our own Centerlines, one characteristic of our lives is accepting a sense of ambiguity. The task before us is to rediscover our sources of strength and integrity, to articulate them, to integrate them, and to live them.

Chapter 28

Self Centerlines

"We must learn to reawaken and keep ourselves awake, not by mechanical aid, but by an infinite expectation of the dawn."

- *Henry David Thoreau*

As we go about our own lives, we use many techniques to rediscover and articulate our sources of strength and integrity. The booming business of life coaches and the multitude of online five-minute personality quizzes all seek to provide us a glimpse into the folds of our own mental kimono. The world of pop psychology makes for countless bestsellers for a great reason: we all are searching and trying to find a way to understand ourselves and others.

There is a variety of techniques that you can use to recognize and link together the competing interests to structure your Centerline. The tool that I, and many others, have used within organizations is that of the Balanced Scorecard. This technique requires a balancing of demands throughout an organization, and includes the creation of linkages. It clearly shows the connections and dependencies among the facets of the organization.

Originally designed in the early 1990s by Drs. Robert Kaplan and David Norton, the Balanced Scorecard is a management and communication tool that allows organizations to recognize numerous, sometimes competing, interests; clarify their vision and strategy; and create a roadmap to bring that vision about.

The principles used to help an organization also can be used to help individuals. In many ways, defining organizations is a much simpler process than understanding ourselves. Organizations have objective criteria; our lives do not.

Nevertheless, while recognizing the innate limitations, we can use a similar approach to create a Balanced Scorecard for the self. Our lives have our beliefs, our dreams, and our visions. We recognize and should continually adjust the balance between multiple aspects, such as relationships, spirituality, physical well-being, and career. Centerlining lets us embrace this notion and find an intrinsic, balanced fulfillment in four major aspects of life initially presented by Shakti Gawain:

- **Relationships:** Forging healthy, respectful, honest, loving, playful, and complementary ones

- **Spiritual:** Developing a sense of self, our ontological relationships, and our unity with God

- **Physical:** Striving for mental and physical well-being and fitness

- **Career:** Embracing a profession that gives us a sense of real achievement and provides long-term value

Relationships   Spiritual   Physical   Career

**FIGURE 14: Components of a
Balanced Scorecard for the Self**

Each of these aspects is important and needs to be routinely nurtured. Each aspect has its own components.

Family · Friends

Relationships

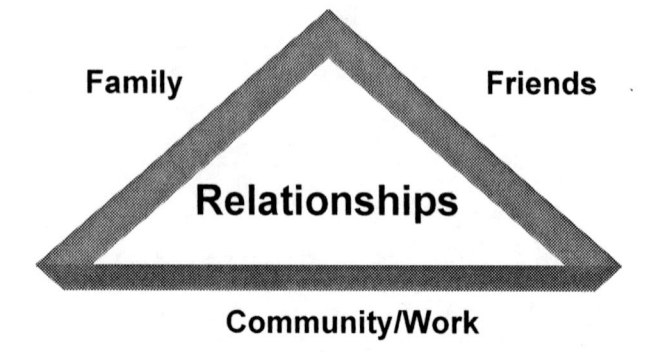

Community/Work

FIGURE 15: Relationship Components

External · Internal

Spiritual

Unity with God

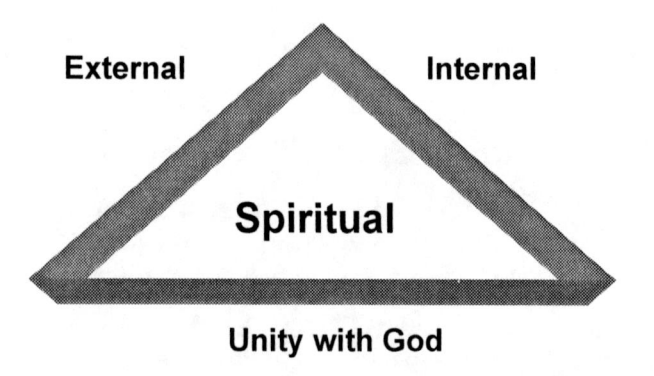

FIGURE 16: Spiritual Components

Mental Well-being | **Physical Well-being**

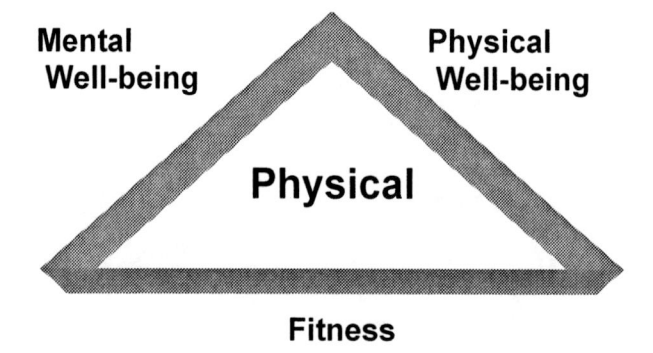

Physical

Fitness

FIGURE 17: Physical Components

Emotional Fulfillment | **Financial Fulfillment**

Career

Long-Term Value

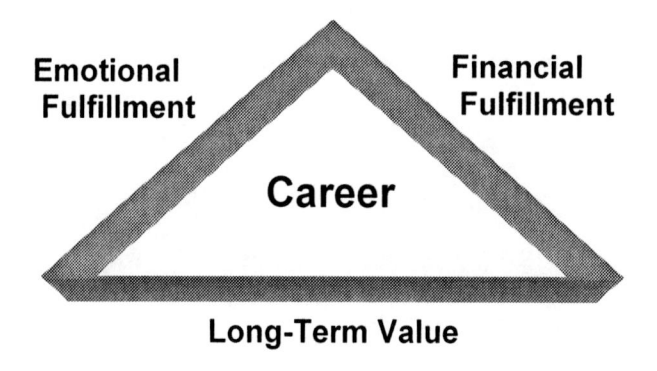

FIGURE 18: Career Components

Each aspect is linked, and activity in one area impacts the others.

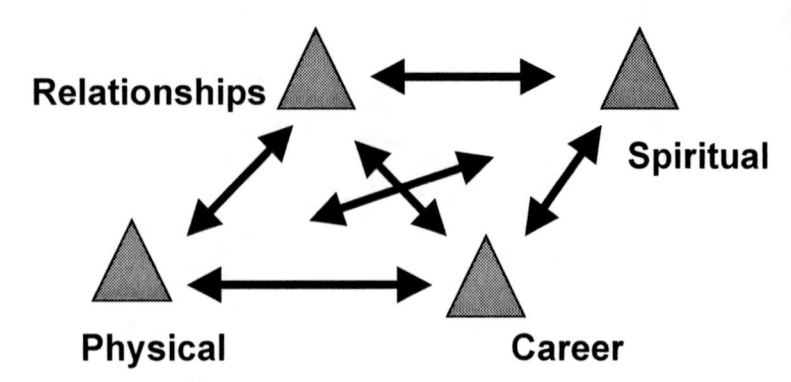

FIGURE 19: Linking the Components

Once we start to understand those aspects of our lives, our own Centerline becomes apparent.

FIGURE 20: Balancing the Components

And, as with any approach, concentrating efforts on one aspect throws the whole out of balance. We see it in couples who no longer have anything in common when their children leave; we see it as our relationships stagnate; we see it as our internal spiritual life turns cold.

This intentional development is difficult. It is easy to get caught up in raising children and forgetting about "date night." It strains us to take in new facts. Many pressures try to prevent our intentionally developing ourselves. However, the lack of balance leads to numbness in life. A focus on a single aspect causes the other aspects to wither and atrophy.

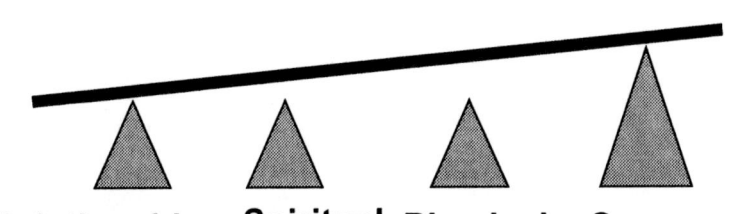

Relationships   Spiritual   Physical   Career

FIGURE 21: Unbalanced Components

This is what our society needs. Recognition of the strength and balance found within a realized Centerline and encouragement to develop this balance. We recognize the impact of our actions and we recognize how all of our actions are linked together. Based on these categories, take a few minutes to re-reflect upon those attributes that you identified earlier in our journey.

Relationship

- Family Influences
- Friends' Influences
- Community Influences
- Work Influences

Spiritual

- External
- Internal
- Unity with God

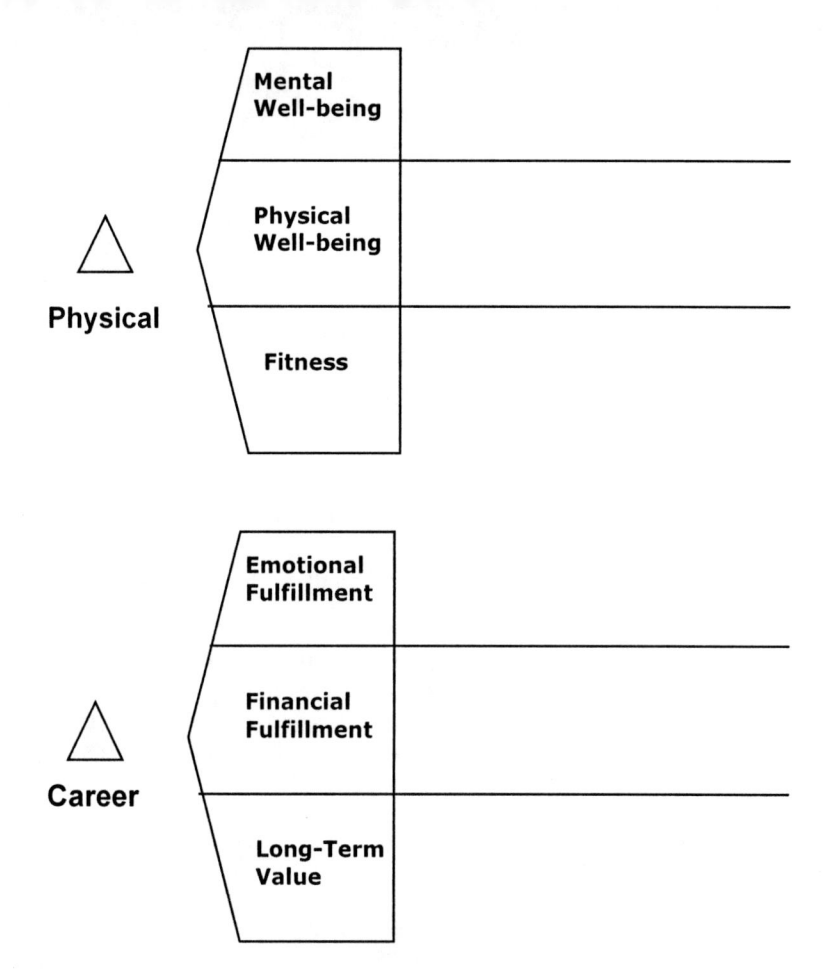

△ **Physical**
- Mental Well-being
- Physical Well-being
- Fitness

△ **Career**
- Emotional Fulfillment
- Financial Fulfillment
- Long-Term Value

FIGURE 22: Identifying Influences

Chapter 29

Organizational Centerlines

"States are not moral agents—people are, and can impose moral standards on powerful institutions."
- Noam Chomsky

We commonly define ourselves by our work. Our public persona is directly tied to what we do. Our waking hours are spent engaged in work. We come to believe that there is an implied social contract between our work place and ourselves.

Then, we remember that corporations are by their very nature amoral. They are not immoral, just amoral. Executives and directors are obligated only to ensure the corporation's long-term viability. Legally they are simply required to return financial profits.

Still, we take our intrinsically moral, holistic selves and try to define ourselves within this amoral, single-focused framework. And we wonder why it doesn't work. Simply put, it can't. It does not make any sense, because it can't make sense. Just as round pegs do not fit into square holes, we can't jam ourselves into this framework.

It does not need to be that way. If corporations have rights within a society, then they should have responsibilities within that society. These are the two sides to society's coin; you can't have one without the other. With some planning and forethought, our workplace, careers, and selves can complement each other.

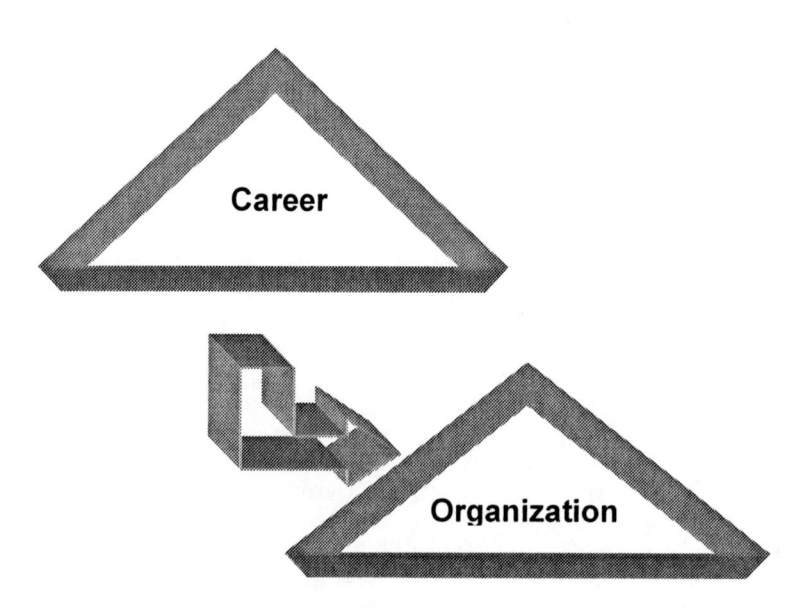

FIGURE 23: The Organizational Subset

Centerlining the workplace and civic organizations provides a framework designed to enable all members to have a way to bring themselves forth routinely. Workplace frameworks can intentionally create opportunities and techniques to allow all to participate and each to fully realize themselves, while still taking into account the organization's vision and bottom line.

I routinely sit with my team members and business partners, look them in the eye, and describe what I think makes them "tick." I try to summarize what I think they value and what they want to get from the business. Further, I also describe how we can get there together, keeping the long-term interests of the organization in mind. Sometimes I'm right on the mark, and other times I am so far off that I question my own judgment. Usually I'm pretty close. This exercise helps me understand my team and remove any hurdles that would prevent us from collectively achieving all of our goals.

Every organization can create and use a Centerline to help it think through its values, explicitly balance competing interests, link them together coherently, continually revalidate them, constantly communicate them, and execute a business strategy that achieves all of its goals. The process examines which business opportunities to explore. It candidly discusses where to spend tax dollars. It establishes whether we are marketplace leaders or followers.

I have spent my recent career at open source start-ups, using leading-edge technologies to create new products and then literally giving them away. I have tried to build an organization that embodied the values I hold dear—honest customer value, fair compensation, and enjoyable and challenging work. I have truly struggled to develop rational business models and value propositions.

To answer these questions and create an organizational Centerline, I used the same Balanced Scorecard approach that I had modified for individual use. Like individual Balanced Scorecards, my organizational Balanced Scorecards concentrate on four major areas. In this instance, these are areas that most in the business community believe critical to ensuring the long-term success of most organizations: Financial, Internal Business Processes, Products & Markets, and Learning & Growth.

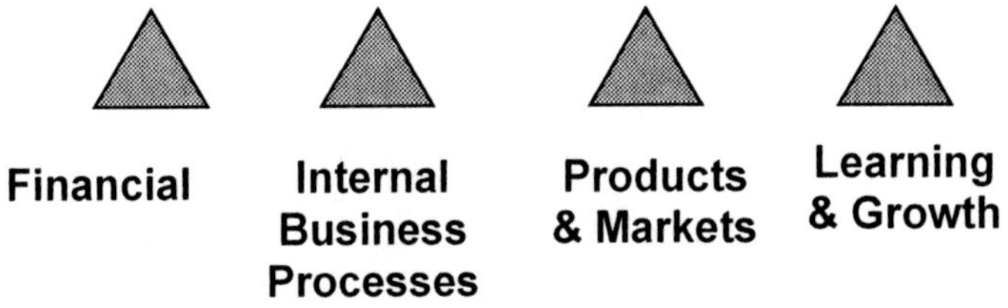

Financial　　Internal　　Products　　Learning
　　　　　　Business　　& Markets　　& Growth
　　　　　　Processes

FIGURE 24: Organizational Balanced Scorecard Components

Within each of these groupings are different components, each of which has to be documented, measured, and reported by the particular organization. These components do not stand by themselves, but contribute to the success of the whole. Each component has its own measurements, targets, and actions. All link to each other and to the whole of the organization. A sample of the components within each of these groups follows.

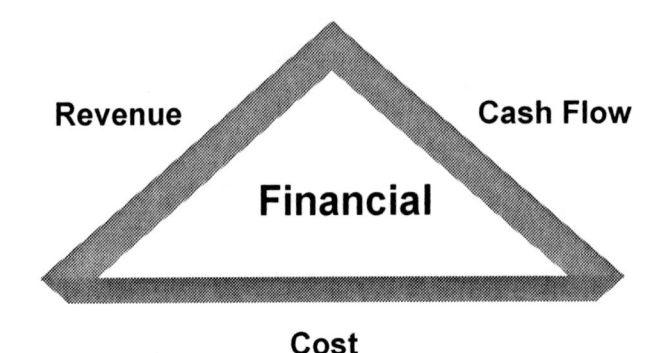

Revenue　　　　　　　　　　　Cash Flow

Financial

Cost

FIGURE 25: Financial Components

Operations

Internal Business Processes

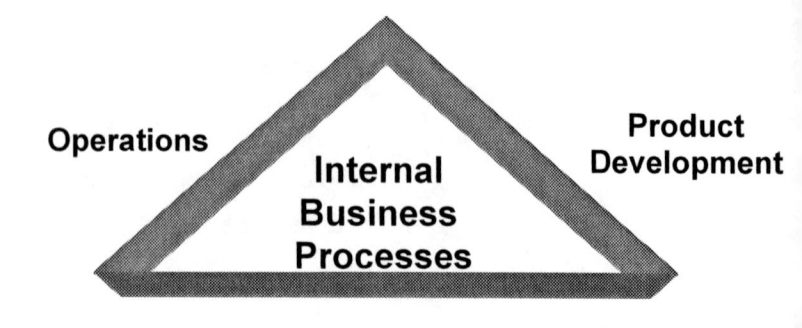

Product Development

Customer Service

FIGURE 26: Business Process Components

Market Share

Products & Markets

Customer Satisfaction

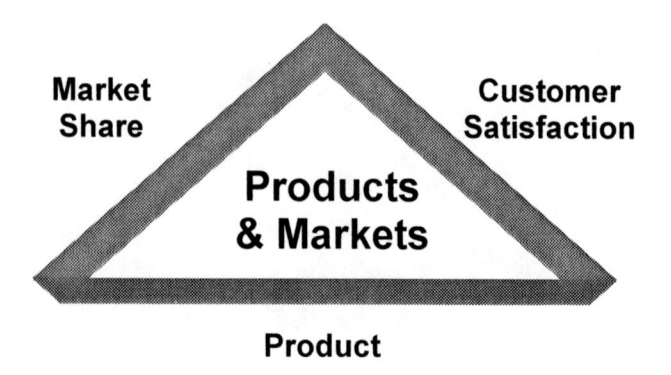

Product

FIGURE 27: Products & Markets Components

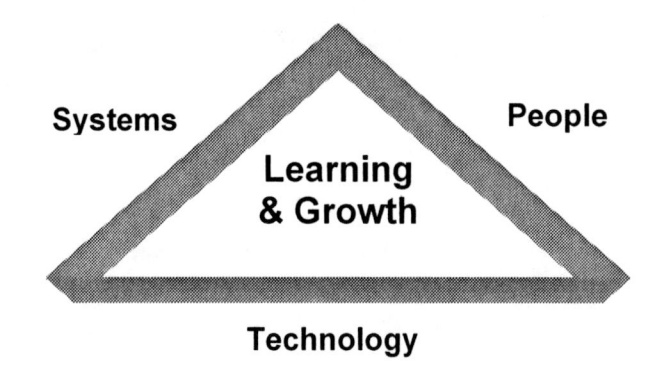

FIGURE 28: Learning & Growth Components

Financial, market, organization, and individual perspectives of the company are reconciled, and feedback is built into the process. Metrics are designed and specified at every level so they can be objectively defined and linked with success from the outset. The feedback cycle allows for intentional changes in goal and objective.

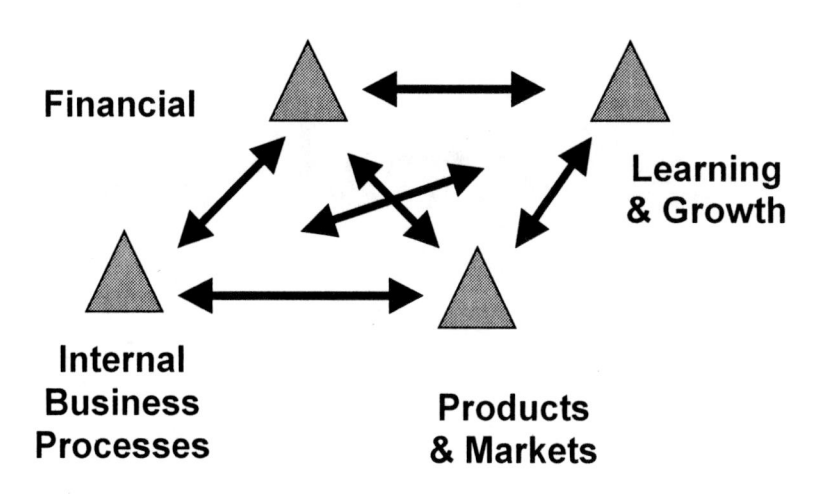

FIGURE 29: Linking Organizational Components

Each of the four areas is explicitly connected and each has to be nurtured for the organization to be truly successful. Everyone within the organization has to buy into it and play together in order for the model to work.

As the goals and vision of the organization are defined, the four areas are balanced and reconciled. The organization's Centerline becomes apparent.

Financial   Internal   Products   Learning
              Business   & Markets   & Growth
              Processes

FIGURE 30: Balancing Organizational Components

Focusing in on one particular area, at least in the long term, causes the organization to lose its balance.

Financial   Internal   Products   Learning
              Business   & Markets   & Growth
              Processes

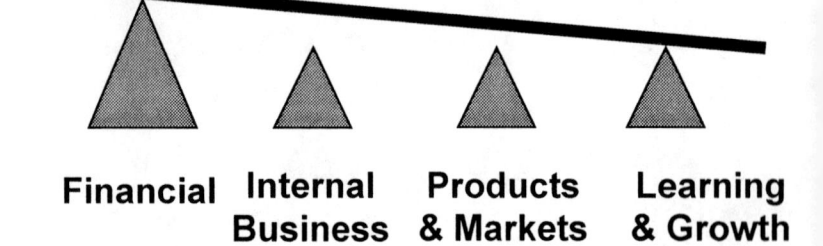

FIGURE 31: Unbalanced Organizational Components

Centerlining does not imply that companies become tools for social welfare programs, but they must ensure that the highest ethical standards are being met. They can have specific programs that help them become socially responsible. This social responsibility does not need to conflict with long-term profitability. Some basic suggestions include: hiring interns; providing college scholarships; funding small seed business and sponsoring business-case competitions; supporting and funding university research related to engineering and key technologies; sending employees to assist at elementary, middle, and high schools; and investing in the local community. I routinely hire interns and have found them a great source for insights and enthusiasm. The University of Pennsylvania has reportedly invested over $1 billion in the area surrounding the school, making that area more livable and sustainable for both the students and the community.

Chapter 30

Communicating Our Centerlines

"Communicating leads to community, that is, to understanding, intimacy, and mutual valuing."
- *Rollo May*

Clear, candid, consistent—these are just some of the components of Centerlined communications. Most of us need to remember how to communicate in an engaged, receptive, reflective fashion. We need to learn how to say what we believe in and why we believe it. We need to learn how to have honest discussions.

As part of my own process, I started using a simple approach many years ago: PLUS. Standing for Pause—Listen—Understand—Speak, the PLUS concept is a way to describe the active listening process. We put aside our tendency to talk immediately and take a pregnant pause. We truly listen to the words and intent, cueing in on verbal and nonverbal signals. We try to understand other perspectives and intentions. Then we speak.

Beyond active listening, part of a Centerlined communications process is the socialization of the Centerline—forced instances with candid interchange. We intentionally create moments to Centerline. This is not the "hucksterism" of marketing. You're not selling or manipulating. You are working toward providing everyone with a common understanding. Focusing communications on your Centerline links each of the pieces with each other with candor and clarity. The process does take time and patience. It is unrealistic to expect immediate changes or comprehension.

In business situations, for Centerlining to actually work, an organization takes a long-term approach as it reaches out to its team members and talks about its Centerline. The communications can be done in a phased approach, soft launched as it were. The objective is to provide information and to promote interaction. Discussions are designed to create a dialogue that allows the corporation to define its climate clearly, to obtain feedback, and to establish methodologies for follow-up. The discussion also allows us to manage expectations. By clearly stating what we can do and why we are doing it, we allow others to understand what results they can expect. We try to remove, or at least minimize, uncertainty.

The next stage is normalizing Centerlined operations. A Centerlined workforce is critical to success in the marketplace and the delivery of high-quality work. One approach is to implement specific policies to create a Centerlined working environment—open communications, clear goals, coherent visions, and explicit rewards and punishments. The new Centerlined standards should be woven into every aspect of the organization's culture.

Communicating your own Centerline is a bit more daunting. As you discover yourself, your traditional social networks may push back. They may not be limber enough to stretch with you.

We can read the inscriptions in our high school yearbooks and think about individuals who have long ago transitioned out of our worlds. We remember friends whom we thought we would grow old with and acknowledge that we don't know them anymore. We leave our home towns, changing in some regards and remaining constant in others. On occasion we return to a world that has also both changed and remained constant. We realize that we have changed; we realize that they have changed. Sometimes, we change in ways that are embraced and sometimes we change in ways that are difficult to accept.

The candor required to tell family, friends, and partners the truth is difficult, because it is personal. You can't hide behind a veil of business goals and objectives nor discount the emotional importance. You do have to face your discomfort and put aside the urge to remain within your safety zone.

At a recent event, I said goodbye to a couple whom I had known for many years and through many experiences. I knew that our goodbye would be our last goodbye; I knew that it would only be by happenstance that I might see them again. Our paths had diverted, and our journeys separated to such an extent that I realized that those things we once had in common had long drifted down different streams. On my way back to my room, I passed a chapel, went in, and cried. My tears were due to sadness and regret.

Our differences were too great. They were resolute, grounded in a belief structure that was not open to a continual revelation. They were fixed in a belief with clearly defined rules and preset outcomes. They were fixed in a belief that did not recognize the paradoxical nature of our journey. We had stopped truly communicating.

Chapter 31

The Centerline Paradox

"Life is a process of becoming, a combination of states we have to go through."

- *Anaïs Nin*

In a society that relishes games with defined rules, we find comfort in straightforward Aristotelian logic—logic that assumes that X and non-X are exclusionary.

For or against, black or white, hot or cold—life would be much easier if only we had such simple polarities upon which to base our decisions. But we already know that life is not that simple. The world is not mutually exclusive.

We know that contradictions are part of our very nature. We have to become comfortable in acknowledging life's grey. We have to learn how to appropriately balance competing interests and values.

In contrast to Aristotelian logic, there is a tradition of paradoxical logic. Paradoxical logic does not assume that X and non-X necessarily exclude each other. This paradoxical logic is part of the foundation of the interpretative process of Centerlining. Life's pendulum constantly swings, and we have to swing with it.

Our Centerlining process causes us to integrate some seemingly opposing positions. We find ways of understanding something in its entirety. We look for a unity of opposites.

Furthermore, this process never comes to a complete close. We are constantly evaluating and revising. As we reach toward one Centerline, we should remain open to new facts and insights.

We struggle as we continually try to make concrete our very intangible thoughts, feelings, and values. We try to objectify these things and give them solid and permanent shapes.

In doing so, we have to have an actual transformation, a process by which we engage every dimension of our being to find that concrete expression. We recognize that behind these fixed and static frameworks are some transcendental, but unknowable, mysteries.

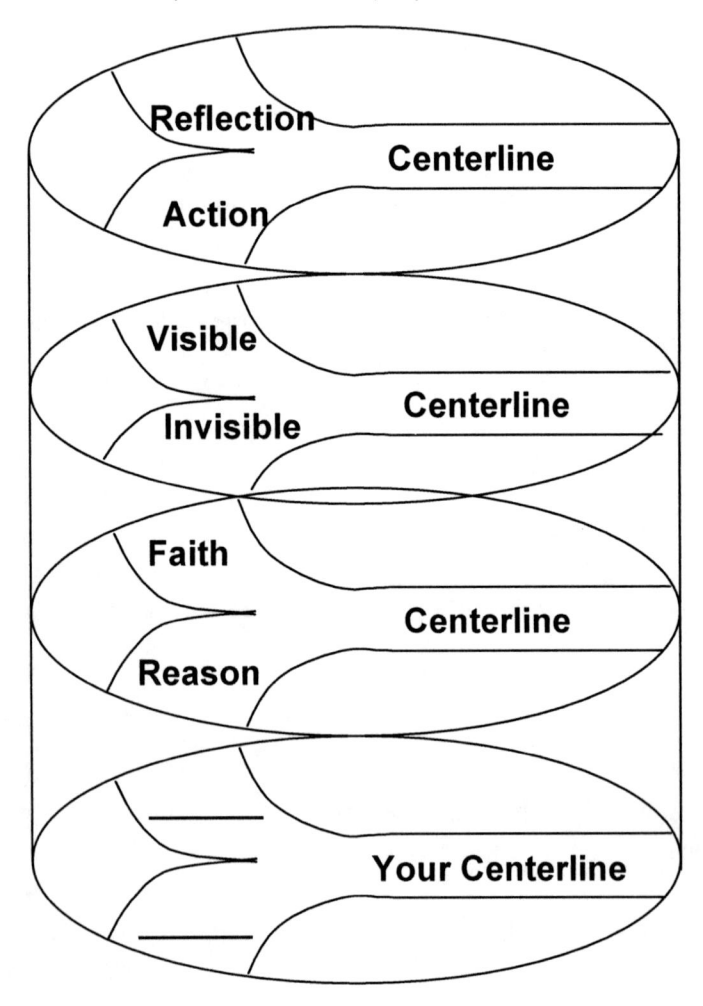

FIGURE 32: Integrating Contradictions

Chapter 32

Centerlined Leadership: No Heroes, Friars, or Lords

"The leaders who do good deeds reside in the hearts of the people."
- Rig Veda

Why do we celebrate dysfunctional leaders? The media gives us role models of businessmen who loot companies or use bankruptcy as a business strategy; we invest in corporations held together not by product or intellectual capital, but by accounting gimmicks; we don't hold politicians accountable for obvious wrongdoings.

We should expect our civic leaders and corporate leaders to have an interest and vision beyond their own particular faction or bottom line. Few people are actually living or actively learning this type of leadership. Our society does not intentionally or consistently produce or promote this type of person.

Tethered by our frames or fears, we become confined within the protective shadows of our own particular walled village. Like vassals of a feudal lord, we don't leave those protective confines. Sadly, there are those who encourage this. They assume or presume "power" based on being the guards of these walls or the lord within. And we let them have it.

In a Centerlined world we don't have these lords; we have coaches. We don't permit heroes to ride in for the rescue but agree to implement smaller, incremental steps toward the mutually agreed goal; we do not have a separate group that bestows a creed but rather each one of us has to understand and embrace the beliefs.

The Centerlined leader has a style that is active, reflective, and unaffected. We are allowed to ask questions and say that we don't know. We expect dissent, disagreement, and truth from those around us. We actively search for the truth by ourselves and with each other.

Respect, but Don't Idolize, Tradition

Orthodoxy and tradition can be tools of power. There is a power of authority bestowed by orthodoxy and an unquestioned acceptance of the slogans and mottos. Centerline's critical reasoning ensures that individuals can't hide behind that screen.

But it doesn't get rid of the traditions and values of the community; it does force us to understand why something happens and doesn't accept that tradition dictates something. As I wrote earlier, we think for ourselves, not by ourselves. We are the product of those who have gone before us.

We can create new traditions. I admit that my favorite holiday is not Christmas. My favorite holiday is Thanksgiving. As opposed to the commercialism surrounding a Coca-Cola stylized Santa Claus, Thanksgiving is a quiet time. A holiday created in a new world, it symbolizes a time for family, fellowship, and reflection. I still vividly remember getting packed into our family car and driving to northern New Jersey for the best meal of the year created by the best chef that I know. My aunt spent hours planning and preparing, scouring countless cookbooks for the perfect recipes. We dressed up, and as we got older, black tie was the norm. We created the special time and place and gave our own meaning to Thanksgiving.

Look Around

A clear Centerline forces an articulation of the organization's mission and measurements of success. It "deglazes" and cleans out the "blah, blah, blah" factor endemic to most organizations. Using a Centerlined approach, we can look team members in the face. A Centerlined leader relishes in and learns from the information gathered by various 360-degree evaluations and customer surveys. We are accessible and provide numerous ways to let others access us.

One of my military reserve jobs was as an Observer-Controller, someone who formally evaluated units. My group prepared units for actual deployment by conducting and evaluating training. To gauge performance and rectify any problems, we routinely conducted After Action Reviews.

These reviews are formally built into essentially every training event done by the Army. Setting aside individual rank, reviews became professional discussions, not critiques. Led by a neutral moderator, the participants focus on the given tasks and the outcome. Late at night, worn from field fatigue, the reviews could become heated, but they could never become personal. We sought to have the participants objectively establish why things happened and how to do the task better the next go around.

As I move into different jobs, I bring some of these techniques with me. I routinely take the pulse of the organization via customer and employee surveys. I allow everyone the ability to provide anonymous feedback. My directors and I have spent full days on the results. Some comments were complaints about service and quality; some comments were compliments about performance. Each of the comments was reflected on. The team came to trust us when they saw real action based on their input.

In the current atmosphere of additional focus on ethics and corporate governance, Centerlining can assist leaders in re-establishing the bridges of trust. If we hold firm to the belief that we all want to act in an ethical fashion, we as Centerlined leaders can concentrate on actually running our government, our businesses, and our lives

Grow Everyone

Centerlined leaders give their team members a chance to grow and learn. They force them to think about what they want their future to be.

We have to mentor everyone around us and play to their strengths. I have tried to engage in active mentorship both formally and informally, internal to my particular group and external to the group. I like to engage in an intentional process of looking someone in the eye and figuring out how to help that person grow, especially if I don't tell the person about what I'm doing.

As a manager, I have my team members write their future résumé, what they want it to look like in five years—long enough to let them dream and short enough to be realistic. It gives us all a chance to develop together, and not merely float along. They are forced to figure out their strengths and weaknesses. They find ways to play to their strengths and passions while mitigating their weaknesses.

One of my managers took this to heart. A great manager to begin with, he began to excel. Eventually, for two years in a row, he was named one of the top five data center managers in the country and had formed this professional organization's fastest-growing chapter.

Open Your Books

Centerlining applies integrity in the ongoing area of financial scandals. Growing up, I spent many hours at an uncle's accounting firm.

I rapidly learned that I was not cut out for accounting. I could not use an adding machine; I was frustrated with double entry bookkeeping and making sure that everything balanced. I think that my ongoing aversion to balancing my checkbook stems from this period.

I did take the time and, with a good deal of patience on my uncle's part, I saw that the mechanics of accounting principles and comprehending spreadsheets can be learned. I did understand that solid accounting principles were straightforward. I was clearly taught that smoothing the numbers to hit the quarterly filing was not appropriate. Simply put, not understanding the company's finances means that you didn't try.

Accountability for All

While Centerlined leaders may not be accountants, they are accountable. Centerlined leaders take accountability for their and their team's actions and do not shy away from hearing ugly news. Not knowing because you didn't want to know the details of an accounting transaction or refused to read an International Committee of the Red Cross report does not preclude complicity.

I remember teaching basic training soldiers the fundamentals of the Laws of Land Warfare—the legal statutes behind ethically conducting war. I instructed Air Force security police officers in the fundamentals of air base ground defense. I used clips from movies such as *Breaker Morant* and *Apocalypse Now* to drive home the point on the right way to treat prisoners.

Set in the early days of the Boer War, *Breaker Morant* dealt with, to paraphrase Winston Churchill, the circumstances of a "new war for a new century." The Boer War is frequently and accurately described as a war with a faceless enemy and with no battle lines. It is a war in which the boundary between friend and foe was completely blurred and harsh methods were the norm. The leader and title character, Breaker Morant, and his men are told that the rules of war no longer apply and that the end justifies the means. The result is disaster. I would contend that the lessons of that time and place directly apply to our "new" war.

Today, we routinely formally evaluate military units on their ability to conduct prisoner of war operations. We know that moving, confining, and treating captured personnel is one of the most difficult military operations. Yet we seemingly didn't realize that this area is one that requires continual focus in real operations. I think that I'm more deeply disturbed than most of us are when I hear the stories of abuse. When we know that a problem exists in the training environment, we know that we need to pay additional attention to those potential problems during actual operations.

When things go wrong, Centerlined leaders take responsibility—they ensure that the resources are available; they intentionally look to ensure that known systematic problems are addressed.

Bottom Line Up Front

Finally, Centerlined leadership does not allow for retrospective justification. There has to be integrity up front. We don't want the rules changed during the middle of the game. To initially justify actions based on one series of "facts," discover the facts to be incorrect, and establish a new justification based on a new series of facts is simply a dishonest rationalization.

Chapter 33

Approaches to Living a Centerline

"Act as if what you do makes a difference. It does."
- William James

As we try to live a Centerlined life, we act with an eye on the "things that matter." We strive to live a life that intentionally balances our relationships, spiritual dimension, physical state, and career. We try to remove the barriers that thwart our ability to balance our paradoxes. We want to balance our attributes, understand our critical issues, see commonality, play to our strengths, and remove the dualism that dominates our lives.

The key to creating a true Centerline is exploring, developing, integrating, and balancing the many facets within us. One of the greatest challenges is to find approaches to integrate into our lives as many of these aspects as possible.

Taking Small Steps

How do we reprogram ourselves and society to Centerline? Positive oral traditions, cultural influences, and intentional actions will allow changes to take root. Repetition and exposure to many small actions and influences is the key to changing from society's current frame to one based more on Centerlined values.

I've been asked to leave only one country, and even then they simply refused to extend my transit visa. Poland in 1983 was a tumultuous place. Train-bound from Beijing through Moscow to meet my brother in Berlin, I spent about a week in Warsaw. The excitement of an impending visit from John Paul II coupled with the vibrancy of my daily participation in the routine Solidarity marches gave me a fleeting taste of the energy of change found within a unified people. By their many small steps, they actively strove to bring forth changes within their world.

Spending 20 Minutes

Distractions are all around us. When do we have time without the clatter of background noise; when do we not feel the draw of the connected world? I can barely remember to take my vitamins each day, much less get the required amount of exercise in.

Yet in the din of the input, we need to touch the quiet spot within. We should recognize the positive value of solitude. Centerlining demands a reflective process. We need the time to develop our mental models.

We all have our transient zones, a time when we are most open to reflection and insight. For me it is the time between being asleep and being awake. It is that short period I use to recharge my interior batteries, to reflect on the lessons of the day, to clear my head of all the noise and to rest simply in God.

In the Christian tradition, this process of Contemplative Prayer is considered to be the gift of pure love from God. As we open our minds and hearts, we can allow our whole being access to God. Through grace, we open our awareness to God. Our daily encounter with God and reflection on His word leads beyond mere acquaintanceship to an attitude of friendship, trust, and love.

There may not be a lot of time each day. There does need to be quality time—time dedicated to reflection intentionally included as part of your routine.

"Just My Corner"

The full phrase is, "I can't change the whole world, just my corner." I can't take credit for this adage, but I vividly remember whom it was credited to—Mother Theresa.

I spent a year of university in Taiwan. Saturday mornings were with the Missionary Brothers of Charity, the male side of Mother's society. We worked in charity wards washing and shaving patients; we worked in a leprosarium doing outreach.

We tried to change only those things immediately around us. We changed only our corner of the world. We spent time with the elderly who had no one else to take care of them; we washed those who would have gone unwashed; we prayed with those who had no other spiritual outlets.

We engaged in the process of a virtuous cycle. We sought only to make small positive changes each day in our own corner. As we changed our corner, those waves of change went forward. Our waves changed others.

Learning to Learn

As we grow in our own experiences, what else happens? Do we forget how to learn or do we simply lose the mental flexibility that children possess? We fall into comfortable patterns and methods. We fit things into our preexisting frameworks without reflection.

In Centerlining, we practice active learning; we don't settle for getting an attendance award. We approach the world with a child's innocence and we cultivate our ability and desire to approach situations with openness.

Growing up, I was blessed with a mother who was a teacher, a teacher of children commonly referred to as those with special needs. There was nothing rote about their learning process. Each student had particular needs, each had his or her own individual development plan, each one learned differently, and each one learned how to learn.

Daily she would return home and relate what she had learned from her students. The lesson could be simply having found a new way to help one student grasp a concept, or some insight that they provided. Daily she was able to learn from her students, her accidental teachers.

Exploring a Third Space

We get caught into the dilemma each day of focusing in on two places that consume so much of our lives—home and work. Each requires us to act in certain fashions and sets certain expectations upon us. Not that we don't enjoy those roles—for if we didn't, we could change them.

Still, where do we find a place to help discover a new self or rediscover an old self? Do you have the ability to find a space outside your home and your workplace that "feels" right? Do you have your coffee shop, community center, diner, library, or social club?

In Washington, D.C., there is a tradition of dining clubs. The dining clubs grew out of a nineteenth-century social convention of letting the house staff have one night off a week. Obviously people had to eat somewhere that night, and a series of private clubs came about to fulfill that need.

A few years ago, I joined one of those clubs, the Arts Club of Washington. Located in one of the power corridors of Washington, the Club owns the house that served as President Monroe's residence until the White House was fully restored from the damage inflicted by the British during the War of 1812.

I am happy to say that this club is unique in the politically-infused world of D.C.; I have no clue what anyone in that club does for a living. Politics is not discussed; work is not discussed; the evening's performance or the current exhibit is the topic of conversation. The club is a place that lets me step out of my normal world and into another.

Doing What Is Simply Right

Centerlining is also doing what is right, merely because it is right. We should not do something because we believe that someone is watching, or that the action may end up in the "A" section of the *Wall Street Journal*. We simply need to do it because it is right.

I was twenty-six when I took my Army company command. For those who have not attended a change-of-command ceremony, it is a big deal. As in a movie setting, the unit forms up in precise ranks. The soldiers and noncommissioned officers are rank and file. Your family, friends, fellow officers, and senior commanders are in attendance. Flags wave all around you. When you take the command, you get the chance to introduce yourself; when you leave the command, you get to bid your farewells.

Almost twenty years later, I have the single index card with my notes from both occasions. The notes state that I wanted my soldiers to do what was right merely because it was right—not because they feared punishment, not because someone was watching. They should do each action merely because it was right.

Now, while not quite *Full Metal Jacket*, this unit was a basic training unit. The drill sergeants did yell, soldiers were intentionally stressed, and there were many times that a simple cutting of a corner could make life much easier—for that moment, but that wouldn't have been right.

Seeing Another

Have you ever run into someone whose life you dramatically impacted and you never even knew it? Conversely, can you point to someone who shifted your life without that person's ever knowing it? Did you ever tell the person? Did he or she ever tell you?

I interviewed for a job about ten years ago in Orlando and went out for a drink afterward. I was sitting in the bar and started talking with one of the other patrons. After the discussion began, I realized that he knew a lot about me—an awful lot about me. Flashing into my mind were clips from Hollywood stalker films.

It's not often that you end up randomly drinking with one of the soldiers that you had put through basic training. I hadn't realized the impression that I had made on him until that night, and then realized that I obviously hadn't realized the impression that I had made on many other of my soldiers. I simply tried to treat them fairly and instill within them a sense of being a soldier.

It's not often that we get the chance to find out how we unintentionally touched someone. But, this night did bring the point home that every encounter, although seemingly insignificant, may have an importance far beyond any so-called reasonable expectation.

I think that encounters like that cause us all to reflect about those who have touched us more significantly than they will ever know. Throughout my years I have been "touched" by some in ways that I have only truly come to appreciate as the years have gone by. Two in particular, vastly dissimilar in profession, bonded by experience, touched me and helped me define the notion of inner strength.

Even as an elderly priest rambling around the parish house, the first one was still an imposing figure. Grey haired, a bit stooped, he had that calm presence that I think every priest aspires to have. His sermons were a bit tough to follow, but our conversations made me stop in my tracks. I had to listen to every word. I learned from his reflective pauses and the spaces between his words.

Father John Clifford, SJ, was a gutsy man. As a younger priest, he had been a prisoner for his faith. In the aftermath of the communist takeover of China, Father Clifford was held in captivity and subjected to years of torture and privation. He literally wrote the book on brainwashing. He gave me my first copy of *In The Presence Of My Enemies*, his seminal work and the basis of a movie with the same name. The true definition of inner strength came through, because he never gave in to the years of privation and torture.

Lieutenant Colonel James "Nick" Rowe was another who suffered through years of abuse and defined inner strength. Held in a bamboo cage, his years as a Vietnam War prisoner were harrowing. The daily barrage of propaganda and threats caused others to break. But his soft-spoken inner strength showed through in his everyday actions. As did Father Clifford, Nick wrote about his experiences. As does Father Clifford's book, Nick's book makes one shudder. I didn't know him nearly as well as I got to know Father Clifford. I did come to respect him and appreciate the advice that he gave me.

I know that neither one of these men ever knew what their words and deeds meant to me. I just wish that I could have told them, and could tell everyone who has impacted me how much he or she really means to me.

Seeing a Platinum Rule

As we try to identify those values that define us, we seem to fall back upon "do unto others as you would like them to do unto you," the Golden Rule. Is it the Golden Rule that we want, or something more?

We should remember the so-called 11th Commandment, "Love thy neighbor as thyself," as our focus for a Centerlined life. The norm of brotherly love goes beyond the ethic of fairness found within the Golden Rule. The Platinum Rule is to love your neighbor, to feel a sense of responsibility for him and to be one with him. The Golden Rule has us respect the rights and feelings of our neighbor, but not to love him.

Fostering Civility

In living our Centerlines, we rediscover civility. We understand that each action matters and each of our actions ripples into someone else. When we act without consideration, we only foster rudeness. We realize that one of the most powerful phrases is "thank you" and we rediscover our civility. Your mother was right: A well-placed "thank you" and a sentence that contains the word "please" does matter.

Being Consistent

A Centerline has a believability component. What you place value in and the way that you express it should be consistent. We like to know where others stand, and others want to know where we stand. If we don't model a steady Centerline, we become inconsistent in our thoughts and actions. Over time and place, we flip-flop.

As we fully establish our Centerline, we avoid sending out mixed messages. When we know ourselves and our Centerline, we create a cohesive message that helps others know how to respond.

When we develop our Centerlines, we reveal our shades and nuances. Conversely, without a developed Centerline, we contradict ourselves, and create internal rooms illuminated by a mental strobe light that displays only fragments and chaos. In the words of an Islamic phrase, "your inside and outside need to be the same."

Consistency does not necessarily lead to rigidity. Consistency built upon a refusal to listen and integrate new facts or ideas, however, is strikingly arrogant and comes close to hubris. Changes and revelations occur and an honest acknowledgement of these is healthy.

John Henry Cardinal Newman was soundly criticized in his own time for what would be considered by many today as flip-flopping. Articles and books berated him for his public declarations of his changing position. He simply described his journey. He simply talked about his continual revelation. He simply acknowledged new insights. He simply showed that he was able to grow in his understanding. His journey gave him new insights, which he internalized and in time externalized in his writings and preaching. He didn't flip-flop; he matured.

Externalizing The Natural Rhyme

Within our climate-controlled, data-driven lives, we lose our sense of connection with the elements and impose our artificial rhythms upon the world. In the process, we lose a part of ourselves.

As evidenced by the current Feng Shui craze, I suspect that I'm not the only one who wants to enjoy the comforts of modern life but also feel the rhythms of the world. In the cold of winter, I anxiously await the first signs of spring. As soon as the weather permits, I drop the roof on my car, relishing the crispness of the air and the smells of the season.

I take the time to see the signs of the season as marked by the produce available in the local roadside and farmers' markets. One type of berry, then another, and then another. Spring onions, replaced by a different vegetable, and then finally by an abundance of fresh tomatoes.

These markets have a nature rhythm, a wonder-filled rhythm that dramatically contrasts our daily experiences. It is a rhythm that we long for, and that we seek.

Chapter 34

Drawing Your Centerline

"The longest journey is the journey inward."
- *Dag Hammarskjöld*

I have been fortunate to have been an active participant in many pivotal world events—from the first street protests in Poland to the stalemate on the Korean DMZ; from the birth of the Internet to cleaning up the dot-com wreckage; from the initial discussion of operations other than war to nights spent doing analysis after 9/11. Long nights spent on a guard post or in a network operations center gave me time to think about some of the questions that trouble us all.

My goal in this was not to write a confessional or a thinly disguised memoir a là Daniel Steele. My goal was to provide a way of looking at and coping with the world. A way grounded in thought and action, a way grounded in the old and the new, a way that allows us to have ethics in action. It is simply our glancing backward and reflecting forward.

The Centerlined model makes simple sense. It lets us recognize the complexities around us, lets us seek to know who we are, recognizes our fundamental similarities with others, and gives us a way to embrace the changes that occur as we go through our particular journey.

As I have noted, the Centerlined approach to life does have some key points:

- Explicitly balancing complex, competing interests
- Integrating and communicating *our* values
- Finding our sense of community, our *"we"*
- Linking ourselves together with commonality and mutual respect
- Grounding our communities in love
- Finding meaningful ways to act

Our lives are a continual journey. We all seek to achieve some semblance of individual and community unity while avoiding the loss of identity in rote uniformity. We fear change but realize that we must have a way to incorporate change within our lives. Centerlining is that pragmatic, but idealistic, approach.

We want to find out what works for us and for others, and in what circumstances. Our questions deserve complete answers. Answers not found on a bumper sticker, but complex and nuanced answers.

Our Centerline gives us a way to balance ourselves and our lives as we create and conserve simultaneously. Our Centerlined legacy resides in the way we have touched others and influenced their lives. We have the chance, if we take it, to embrace commonality and ground ourselves in a sense of love. We can draw our own masterpiece by our daily actions rather than simply doodling away our lives.

Works Consulted

In the interest of candor, I have to admit that I have a tendency to consume books. I owe an enormous intellectual debt to many people. I have included the major works that influenced this piece. However, I suspect that I may unintentionally have omitted someone—and for that I apologize.

Arendt, Hannah, *The Origins of Totalitarianism* (New York, New York: Harcourt Brace Jovanovich, 1968)

Arkoun, Mohammed, *The Unthought in Contemporary Islamic Thought* (London, England: Saqi Books, 2002)

Armstrong, Karen, *The Battle for God* (New York, New York: Random House, 2000)

Avineri, Shlomo, *Hegel's Theory of the Modern State* (New York, New York: Cambridge University Press, 1972)

Barnet, Sylvan, Berman, Morton, Burto, William, *Aspects of the Drama* (Boston, Massachusetts: Little, Brown, and Company, 1962)

Beck, John C., Wade, Mitchell, *Got Game* (Boston, Massachusetts: Harvard Business School Press, 2004)

Bennis, Warren, *Why Leaders Can't Lead* (San Francisco, California: Jossey-Bass Publishers, 1990)

Berstein, Richard J., *Praxis and Action* (Philadelphia, Pennsylvania: University of Pennsylvania Press, 1971)

Blanchard, Kenneth and Norman Vincent Peale, *The Power of Ethical Management* (New York, New York: Fawcett Crest, 1988)

Bolinger, Dwight, Sears, Donald, *Aspects of Language* (New York, New York: Harcourt Brace Jovanovich, Inc., 1968)

Carney, John, Editor, *Eyewitness To History* (New York, New York: Avon Books, 1987)

Cassirer, Ernst, *An Essay On Man* (New Haven, Connecticut: Yale University Press, 1962)

Chordron, Pema, *The Places That Scare You* (Boston, Massachusetts: Shambhala Classics, 2002)

Coles, Robert, *The Moral Intelligence of Children* (New York, New York: Random House, 1997)

Covey, Stephen R., *The 7 Habits of Highly Effective People* (New York, New York: Free Press, 1989)

Dallmayr, Fred, *Alternative Visions* (Lanham, Maryland: Rowman & Littlefield, 1998)

De Mello, Anthony, *Awareness* (New York, New York: Image [Doubleday] 1990)

Dörner, Dietrich, *The Logic of Failure* (New York, New York: Metropolitan Books, 1996)

Ebenstein, William, *Today's ISMS* (Englewood Cliffs, New Jersey: Prentice-Hall, 1973)

Fairhurst, Gail T. and Robert A. Sarr, *The Art of Framing* (San Francisco, California: Jossey-Bass, 1996)

Feiler, Bruce, *Abraham* (New York, New York: Harper Collins Publishers, 2004)

Fung Yu-lan, *A Short History of Chinese Philosophy* (New York, New York: MacMillian Company, 1949)

Furedi, Frank, *Culture of Fear* (New York, New York: Continuum Books, 1997)

Gawain, Shakti, *Creating True Prosperity* (Novato, California: Natarj Publishing, 1997)

Hamer, Dean, *The God Gene* (New York, New York: Anchor Books, 2004)

Hicks, John, *The Fifth Dimension* (Oxford, England: Oneworld Publications, 1999)

Hoffer, Eric, *Reflections on the Human Condition* (New York, New York: Harper Row, 1973)

Hoffer, Eric, *The True Believer* (New York, New York: Harper & Row, 1966)

Jefferson, Thomas, *The Jefferson Bible* (Boston, Massachusetts: Beacon Press, 1989)

Johannson, Frans, *The Medici Effect* (Boston, Massachusetts: Harvard Business School Press, 2004)

Jones, Alexander, Editor, *The Jerusalem Bible* (Garden City, New York: Doubleday and Company, 1968)

Kaelin, Eugene F., *An Existential Aesthetic, The Theories of Sartre and Merleau-Ponty* (Madison, Wisconsin, The University of Wisconsin, 1962)

Kelly, George, *Hegel's Retreat From Eleusis* (Princeton, New Jersey: Princeton University Press, 1979)

Low, Douglas, *Merleau-Ponty's Last Vision* (Evanston, Illinois: Northwestern University Press, 2000)

MacIntrye, Aladair, *After Virtue* (Notre Dame, Indiana: University of Notre Dame Press, 1981)

MacIntrye, Aladair, *Three Rival Versions of Moral Enquiry* (Notre Dame, Indiana: University of Notre Dame Press, 1990)

Manji, Irshad, *The Trouble With Islam* (New York, New York: St. Martin's Press, 2003)

Mapp Jr., Alf, *The Faiths of Our Fathers: What America's Founders Really Believed* (Lanham, Maryland: Rowman & Littlefield Publishers, 2003)

Marion, Jim, *Putting on the Mind of Christ* (Charlottesville, Virginia: Hampton Road Publishing Company, 2000)

May, Rollo, *Man's Search For Himself* (New York, New York: Dell Publishing Company, 1953)

Merton, Thomas, *The Seven Storey Mountain* (New York, New York: Harcourt Brace Jovanovich, 1948)

Mintzberg, Henry, *Managers Not MBAs* (San Francisco, California: Brett-Koehler, 2004)

Needleman, Jacob, *Lost Christianity* (New York, New York: Tarcher/Penguin Edition, 2003)

Pagels, Elaine, *Adam, Eve and the Serpent* (New York, New York: Vintage Books, 1988)

Pagels, Elaine, *The Gnostic Gospels* (New York, New York: Vintage Books, 1979)

Rudoph, Kurt, *Gnosis, The Nature & History of Gnosticism* (New York: New York, Harper & Row, 1987)

Sinkinson, Christopher, *the universe of faiths* (Waynesboro, Georgia: Paternoster Press, 2001)

Tablot, John Michael, *The Music of Creation* (New York, New York: Jeremy P. Tarcher/Penguin, 1999)

Taylor, Charles, *Hegel and Modern Society* (New York, New York: Cambridge Press, 1979)

Unger, Roberto, *Knowledge and Politics* (New York, New York: Free Press, 1975)

Welch, Holmes, *The Parting of the Way* (London, England: Meuthuen and Company, 1957)

Wilber, Ken, *A Brief History of Everything* (Boston, Massachusetts: Shambhala Press, 2000)

Acknowledgements

"Each friend represents a world in us, a world not possibly born until they arrive, and it is only by this meeting a new world is born."
- *Anaïs Nin*

It is tough to thank everyone who helped me through this journey. I have been fortunate to have had many personal, professional, and intellectual mentors in my life. Each one of them has caused a wave that rippled through me, and I hope that I have been able to make them proud as I have tried to incorporate those waves.

For the inspiration, my nieces Julia, Charlotte, Grace, Maeve, Dorothy, and Sarah. For his intellectual mentorship, Fred Dallamyr. To Susan Watterson for her inspirational cooking. To Robert Stewart for his ability to make a glass of wine come alive. To Steve Basdavanos for his unique ability to rail at me about art.

My special thanks go to my editors Susan Christophersen, Jennifer Kirkland and Sheila Schroeder, who captured the essence of what I was trying to say; the team at DogEar Publishing, who helped me through this process; my friend Rolf Purzer, who introduced me to the Balanced Scorecard; and my friend Phyllis Andes, whose advice ensured that I had the time to write.

My profound thanks goes to all of those who read the galleys and put up with me as I wrote this: my friends and colleagues at Open Travel Software, the Defense Information Systems Agency and the Arts Club of Washington, Father Pat Neary, CSC, Father PJ Frances, SJ, Father Jim Heyd, Richard Guther, Edward Shaw, Steve Clemmons, Andrew Oros, Warren Coats, Victorino (Ito) Briones, Stan James, Stephanie Paige, Frances Ellis, Doug Dixon, Alfred Rivera, Rolf and Juana Purzer, Wendy Gordon, Bob Sacheli, Ben Carver, Mike Nichols, Tom Zellars, Russ Webber, David and Laurie Mastic, Will Bower,

Kevin Wells, Tony Stanco, Scott Mendenhall, Carter and Jennifer Lane, Andy and Marlene Tucker, Pattie Buel, Jim Flahive, Michael Sullivan, David Sossoman, Jason DeMoranville, David Jones, Dorinda Smith, Mike Kirk, Roberta Osborn, Florence and Ed Wallace, my brothers Robert and John, my sisters Elise and Kim, my mother, and Jeffrey Brady.

My deepest gratitude goes to my family and friends. They have inspired me, challenged me, forced me to look at myself, and helped me to grow.

About The Author

Henry J. Sienkiewicz graduated from the University of Notre Dame with a Bachelor of Arts degree and from the Johns Hopkins University with a Master of Science degree. He also attended the National Taiwan University.

Commissioned an Infantry Second Lieutenant upon college graduation, he subsequently transferred into the Signal Corps. At the mid-point of his military career, he transferred into the Army Reserves to pursue a civilian career. He has had assignments throughout the world and at every level from platoon leader through Joint Command. He currently holds the rank of Lieutenant Colonel in the United States Army Reserves.

In the corporate world, Henry has been focused on information technology support for the government and aviation sectors. Directly reporting to either the CEO or COO for three different companies, he has helped develop and implement business and complex information technology strategies; he has also helped start and run three different companies. His focus has been on implementing emerging technologies into large, complex operational environments. He is currently the founder and CEO of Open Travel Software, an open source software applications development company.

He has or has had professional and personnel memberships in organizations such as the National Associate of Corporate Directors, the Society for Corporate Secretaries & Governance Professionals, *CIO Magazine*'s CIO Executive Council, the Society For Human Resources Management, the Armed Forces Communications Electronics Association, the National Eagle Scout Association, and the Arts Club of Washington.

He resides in Alexandria, Virginia, and Sarasota, Florida.

Disclaimer

It should go without saying that the views expressed here represent my views and do not necessarily represent the views of any organization with which I am affiliated. But that's not the case, so, I'm saying it: The views expressed here are my own.

Discussion Group Questions

How can you develop a community committed to a continuous cycle of reflection and self-critical activity? Describe some concrete steps.

Discuss a time when the medium, the package, overwhelmed the message?

What is your elevator pitch?

Do your family gatherings revert to the re-enactment of previous events?

What are your "Koans for today?"

Have you ever had a time when you were an outsider? How did it feel? How did you "get through it?"

Have you ever gone through your own "Dark Night of the Soul?" When, and what was the result?

Today, how did you find a way to connect with a stranger?

Where is your own Third Place? How did you find it? Do you share it?

What is your ghetto? And how can you step out of it?

What activities consume your day? What actions should consume your day?

Describe the riskiest thing you have done and why you did it.

Which category of fear is in the forefront of your life, and why?

How does your expression of faith exemplify the virtue of pure love?

Describe the points within your own Balanced Scorecard. Which area is unbalanced?

Where is your organization unbalanced?

How do you describe your own communications style? What event strained your style the most?

What are four (4) approaches you use to live your Centerline?

Name one person you believe is a Centerlined leader and why.

Book Orders

Centerlined can be ordered online through Amazon (www.amazon.com), Barnes & Noble (www.bn.com), or directly from the author (www.centerlined.com).

Index

A
Abrahamic faiths, 60
Abraham (prophet), 54–55
absolutism, 8
accountability, 90–91
action, 86
  meaningful, 94–95, 101
  as purpose driven, 46–47
  and risk, 48
active
  learning, 95
  listening, 82
activity as diversion, 46
Addams, Jane, 46
agape, 63
alienation, 3
analysis paralysis, 44–45
Apocalypse Now (movie), 91
Arendt, Hannah, 24
Arkoun, Mohammed, 60
Arts Club of Washington, 96
Augustine, Saint, 12, 32
Aung San Suu Kyi, 48
Ausländer identity, 25
authoritarianism, 8

B
Balanced Scorecard (Kaplan and Norton)
  balanced/unbalanced, 70–71
  organizational, 75–80
  overview, 66–70
balance points, 25–26, 27
balancing, 25–26, 27, 66–71, 75–80, 101, 102
Bergson, Henri, 57
Berlin, Isaiah, 23
Bible, Christian, 59–60
  Jefferson re-editing, 62
Boer War, 91

Boethius, 19
Bradbury, Ray, 48
Breaker Morant (movie), 91
Brooke, Rupert, 24
Buddha, 61
Buddhism, 55
business process components, 78, 79, 80

C
career, organizational Centerlines, 74–81
career components, 67, 69, 70, 73
  business process components, 78, 79, 80
  ethical standards, 84
  financial components, 77, 79, 80
  learning/growth components, 78, 79, 80
  product components, 78, 79, 80
Catholic Church, 56, 60
Centerline
  beyond home/work, 95–96
  contradiction integration, 86
  life based on, 93–100
  paradox of, 85–86
Centerlining
  balancing worldview, 36
  changing one's "corner," 94–95
  and codification, stepping aside from, 30
  commonality points, 34–36
  communicating of own Centerline, 83–84
  comparing with others, 32–33
  and Contemplative Prayer, 94
  elevator pitch creation, 17
  frames, 16–18
  growth/reframing, 19
  interaction promotion, 83
  long-term approach, 82–83
  with "mental cat paws," 24
  normalizing of, 83
  as ongoing, 85–86
  organizational, 7, 76–80
  overview, 3–4
  by perspective changes, 24
  questions to ask, 17
  reflective regimen, 94
  right doing, 96–97

   rules, 65
   of self (*See* Self Centerlines)
   self-recognition, 28–29
   by small steps, 93–94
   and truth telling, 52
   for workforce, 83
Cervantes, Miguel de, 8
chaos theory, 36. *See also* fractals
Chomsky, Noam, 40, 74
Christian Bible, 59–60
   Jefferson re-editing, 62
Christianity, 60
Christ/Jesus, 55, 61
Churchill, Winston, 91
Cicero, 34
civic organization Centerlines, 75
civic organizations. *See also* organizational Centerlines
civility, 99
clarity. *See* translucence; transparency
Clausewitz, Karl von, 16
Clifford, Father John (SJ), 98
codification, stepping aside from, 30
commonalities, 32–33, 34–36. *See also* community
   and continual revelation, 58
   of faiths, 55
   finding, 39
   of love, 101
   and overcoming egotism, 41
   searching for, 37–38
   of understanding, 82
communication
   active listening, 82
   with candor, 83
   messages that work, 6
   PLUS (Pause—Listen—Understand—Speak), 82
   stoppage, 84
   transparency need, 51–52
   of vision, 2
community. *See also* commonalities
   balancing, 68, 70
   early Christian, 60
   finding sense of, 4
   grounding, 101
   of inquiry, 8
   roots in, 2

synchronizing of, 33
  values, 88
company Centerlining. *See* career components
components. *See* career components; life components
"Connections" (PBS/Learning Channel), 34
consistency, 99–100
Contemplative Prayer, 94
Creating True Prosperity (Gawain), 28
Creeds, 13, 23

D

"Dark Night of Soul," 30
Dead Sea Scrolls, 59–60, 62
discussion questions, 113–114
Disney organization, 12

E

Electrical Code, National, 23
elevator pitch creation, 17
Emerson, Ralph Waldo, 54
Epictetus, 28
eros, 62, 63
ethical standards, 84

F

factionalism, 42–43
faith, 86
  conflicts, 54
  universal similarities, 55
fears, letting go of, 48–49
Feng Shui, 100
financial components, 77, 79, 80
fractals, 21, 26, 61. *See also* chaos theory
frameworks. *See also* roles
  brittle, 58, 61
  Centerline establishment, 6
  closed, 58, 59
  of differing faiths, 55
  establishing, 12–13
  modification, 18
framing
  defined, 12
  of Disney organization, 12, 16

freezing, 19
as influential, 13–15
reframing, 19
self-awareness of, 9–11
societal, 16–18
"Friendster" Web site, 36
Fromm, Eric, 44
Full Metal Jacket (movie), 97

G
Gawain, Shakti, 28
  life aspects, 67
Gibran, Kahlil, 42
The Glass Bead (Hesse), 43
God
  as communal, 54
  grace of, 55
Golden Rule, 98–99
Grace, Divine, 55, 63
grounding
  of Centerline, 54–56
  of communities, 4, 101
  points, 22, 23, 27
  of risk, 48
growth/learning components, 78, 79, 80

H
Habermas, Jürgen, 35
hajj, 55
Hammarskjöld, Dag, 19, 24, 101
heart, unveiling of, 31
Hegel, Georg, 36
Hesse, Herman, 43
hierarchies, traditional, 5
Hinduism, 55
Hoffer, Eric, 25
honesty. *See* truth telling

I
idolatry of surety, 59
Ijtihad, 60
insecurities. *See* fears
insight

  contextual, 22
  fractal, 21, 26, 61
  surface *versus* depth, 21–22
integrating principles/actions, 3, 101
integrity, 91–92
interests
  competing, 5
  linking, 6
Islam, 30–31, 55
  "Golden" Era, 60
  Ijtihad, 60
  Shariah, 60

J
James, William, 93
Jefferson, Thomas, 62
Jesus/Christ, 55, 61
John of the Cross, Saint, 30
journey, personal, 7
justification, retrospective, 91–92

K
Kabbalists, 62
Kaplan, Robert, 66
keys to Centerlined life, 4
kingdom of heaven
  within, 63–64
Koans for today, 24

L
leadership
  accountability, 90–91
  Centerlined style, 87–88
  dysfunctional role models, 87
  and evaluations, 88
  integrity, 91–92
  and justification, retrospective, 91–92
  and mission analysis, 88–89
  respect without idolization, 88
  responsibility taking, 91
  and tradition creation, 88
  trust building, 88–89
  when things go wrong, 91

learning, active, 95
life components. *See also* career components
  identification, 7, 9–11
  linkage, 7
  physical components, 67, 69, 70, 73
  relationship components, 67, 68, 70, 72
  spiritual components, 67, 68, 70, 72
life's journey, 102
listening, active, 82
"Liturgy of the Hours," 55
love
  categories, 62–63
  and centerlining, 61, 101
Love Your Neighbor as Yourself, 62

M
Machiavelli, Niccolò, 39
Marion, Jim, 30
May, Rollo, 82
McCarthy, Mary, 24
McSpirituality, 31
The Medici Effect (bestseller), 34
Merleau-Ponty, Maurice, 36
messages that work, 6
Michener, James, 30
microculture, personal, 16–17
military reserve mobilization, 1–2
Missionary Brothers of Charity, 94–95
Mohammad, 61
Mother Theresa, 94
Muhammad, 55
multi-polarity, 8

N
natural world, 100
Newman, John Henry (Cardinal), 37, 100
Nin, Anaïs, 4, 24, 85, 107
Norton, David, 66

O
O'Neill, Tip, 16
organizational Centerlines, 7
  Balanced scorecard, 76–80

corporation societal rights, 74
organizational subset, 75

P
Pause—Listen—Understand—Speak (PLUS), 82
personal discovery space, 95–96
phileo, 62, 63
physical components, 67, 69, 70, 73
Picasso, Pablo, 1
Pierce, Charles, 8
pigeonholing, 19
pivot points, 25, 27
Platinum Rule, 98–99
PLUS (Pause—Listen—Understand—Speak), 82
politics
　and factionalism, 42
　and fear, 50
　as "we," 42–43
Popper, Karl, 35
pragmatics, 8
Prayer, Contemplative, 94
priorities
　competing, 5
　linking, 6
prisoner of war operations, 91
product components, 78, 79, 80
Putting on the Mind of Christ (Marion), 30

Q
questions
　for discussion groups, 113–114
　and orthodoxy, 88
　of others, 61
　right to, 8
　of self, 75
　value of, 58

R
rationalization, 19
reason, 86
reference points, 23, 27
reflection. *See also* self-reflection
　daily, 94

points, 23–24, 85–86
reflection points, 27
Reformation/Counter-Reformation, Christianity, 60
relationship components, 67, 68, 70, 72
revelation, continual, 57–58, 60
Rig Veda, 87
risk taking, 48
role models/modeling, 97–98
roles, 19. *See also* rationalization
Rowe, James (Lt. Col.), 98
rules, 65
Rumi, 62
Russell, Bertrand, 54

S
self Centerlines
  techniques, 66–67
  and work, 74
self-reflection, 22. *See also main heading* reflection
  as analysis paralysis, 44–45
  daily, 94
  set points, 23–27 (*See also main heading* set points *for details*)
set points, 28–29
  balance points, 25–26, 27
  grounding points, 23, 27
  and perspective, 24, 27
  pivot points, 25, 27
  reference points, 23, 27
  reflection points, 23–24, 27
Shariah, 60
Siddhartha Gautama, 65
Sienkiewicz, Henry J., 109
socialization, 36, 39, 44–45
social responsibility, 84
societal frames, 16–18
spiritual components, 67, 68, 70, 72
Strachey, James, 24
Sufis, 30–31, 62
superficial style, 37

T
Taoism, 36
Third Place recreation, 40–41

Thoreau, Henry David, 66
Tocqueville, Alexis de, 25
tradition creation, 88
translucence, 53
transparency
  need for, 51–52
  overdone, 53
The True Believer (Hoffer), 25
truth telling, 52

U
U.S. Central Command, 53

V
Voltaire, 59

W
Web sites
  "Friendster," 36
wheat from chaff, 5
white noise, 5
Wilber, Ken, 35
Woolf, Virginia, 51
workplace Centerlines, 75. *See also* organizational Centerlines
Worldview Triangle, 35

Printed in the United States
60779LVS00001BF/229-408